A DETESTED
OCCUPATION?

A Detested Occupation?

A History of Domestic Servants
in North Wales 1800-1930

Annie Williams

Thanks

My thanks for their love and support to Paul, my partner and best friend, and Sophie, my lovely daughter; to my grandson Lewis for sharing fun, love and joy. My dear family and friends are far too numerous to mention by name but a collective thank you goes out to you all for always being there. To Neil for everything that he's done for Welsh history and for the friendship and kindness he has shown me over many years. Finally, Myrddin ap Dafydd at Gwasg Carreg Gwalch for supporting the publication of this work.

First published in 2016

© Annie Williams

© Gwasg Carreg Gwalch 2016

Published with the financial support
of the Welsh Books Council

ISBN: 978-1-84527-556-3

Cover design: Welsh Books Council

Published by Gwasg Carreg Gwalch,
12 Iard yr Orsaf, Llanrwst, Wales LL26 0EH
tel: 01492 642031
fax: 01492 641502
email: books@carreg-gwalch.com
website: www.carreg-gwalch.com

I Meirwen,
fy annwyl chwaer fawr

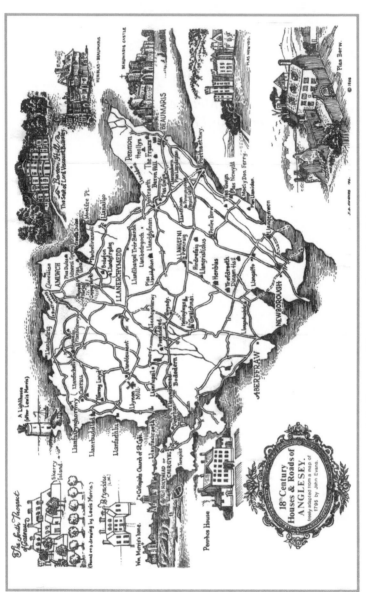

18th Century Houses and Roads of Anglesey

Contents

Introduction

In the light of the recent upsurge in period dramas on film and television and the popularity of programmes like 'Downton Abbey' and on-going repeats and remakes of 'Upstairs Downstairs', it seemed an appropriate time to explore the reality of life for domestic servants in Wales.

Film and television dramas generally present a nostalgic and romanticised view of the nineteenth century seen through the eyes of a paternalistic aristocracy served by a hard working servant class. Servants are presented within a hierarchical structure with all the associated scheming and intrigue that goes on between them.

The remoteness of the aristocracy from their servants is represented by different settings, upstairs and downstairs – one palatial and the other spartan. The harshness and relentlessness of the tasks performed by servants is often well presented but employers are often portrayed as caring individuals and servants generally treated with a degree of fairness and compassion. They eat well and spend some social time together in the servants' hall.

The drama centres on the lives and loves of the people who live under the same roof but inhabit completely different worlds. Dramatic possibilities develop as these worlds intersect through relationships and the events, both mundane and exceptional, that take place in the household. In this world, people know their place and what is expected of them. Class distinctions are clear and consistently reinforced as the drama unfolds.

We are drawn to these dramas because they are seen to represent a time in the past when a clear order existed in society and people knew where they stood within it –

'knowing your place'. Work in the 'big house' is presented as the typical setting for domestic service with its attendant intrigues between 'upstairs and downstairs'. Watching these dramas we are presented with an idealised and romantic view of the past and domestic service is seen as something that happened a long time ago and the pictures we have in our minds of domestic servants in their uniforms will be taken from this time.

The dramas we see on television and film are generally well researched but their scope is narrowly defined around the lives of the most affluent class in the society of the time. It is the task of the historian to question some of these assumptions and consider how representative these images are of life for the majority.

It will be demonstrated here that domestic service for the majority in Wales was far removed from the world presented on television. Most servants were employed in households employing one or two servants and their experience was very much harsher than the world we see in the homes of the wealthy classes. Young girls as young as twelve could end up in single servant households and their experience of loneliness and isolated must have been heartbreaking.

Evidence from the Anglesey Petty Sessions records will show what life was like for servants living in farming communities and how they often found themselves in difficult circumstances. A significant number of women, particularly, very young women, were also employed by family members or friends of family. We will see the tragedies that sometimes occurred when young women were employed in family situations, for example, upon the death of a sister, often in childbirth, when they were expected to perform all the functions of the deceased wife. This often led to the young woman becoming pregnant and the records show that the morality of the time led the putative father to deny responsibility causing the young women herself to carry the burden and shame that was attached at the time to giving birth out of wedlock. These are truly tragic tales.

Although not a concern here as such, the importance of questioning the myth about domestic service has a relevance for contemporary society. The idea that domestic service is a thing of the past and bound to the nineteenth century image of mistresses and their servants in Victorian and Edwardian settings, is clearly untrue. Women servants were hidden from view in the nineteenth century and remained stubbornly outside the influence of trades unionism and legislation that protects workers from exploitation because of the 'private' nature of the work.

The same applies today for the new armies of servants who are employed as nannies, au pairs and domestics on the edges of legality for a new class of the wealthy. Domestic service in the nineteenth century is story of class division, privilege for the few and servitude, hardship, loss of potential, sacrifice and loneliness for the thousands of women who have been hidden from history for far too long. The uniforms may have gone now , but servitude is servitude whatever the setting and understanding what life was like for domestic servants in the nineteenth century should alert us to reality of life for servants today – even now hidden and beyond the bounds of legislation and protection.

This book will show that the wealthy estates did not generally employ local women, particularly in higher ranking roles so the images in drama certainly did not apply in this part of Wales. Hidden behind the veil of respectability that was created by nineteenth century domestic ideology lie the unheard stories of women who were invisible in their time and subsequently in the written history of the period. This is an attempt to give them a voice.

Chapter 1

The Domestic World in the Nineteenth Century

The information in this book is based primarily on original research carried out on servants working in different sized households in Anglesey in the nineteenth century and supplemented by evidence taken from other sources. The work of other historians is used to contextualise the findings from Anglesey and for comparisons within Wales some references are made to the Erddig estate, near Wrexham and Penrhyn Castle in Bangor.

A period that has been described as the 'Industrial Revolution' forms the backdrop to the discussion about servants. This was a time when fundamental changes took place in the organisation of work and the structure of family life. Domestic service was a central feature of society during the nineteenth century and the duties performed by servants were wide ranging. For this reason, it is important at the outset to set boundaries around what categories of servant will be considered here.

The meaning of the term 'domestic servant' changed during the course of the nineteenth century. Because 'service' as a broad category included men and women, it was not defined primarily as a female occupation. This was to change during the course of the century as roles became more differentiated and specialised within the domestic sphere and became a predominantly female occupation.

For clarification the category of servants covered here will be those that were employed in the home of their employer. Other classes of workers such as charwomen, washerwomen and 'daily' domestics who are strictly included within the Domestic Service sector, in general terms, will be excluded. However, for statistical purposes it is not always possible to maintain such a division between these categories of workers.

The historian Lynne Haims has stressed the importance of domestic service as an occupation for women and she has drawn up figures to illustrate this point which show that out of 2,858,576 working women in England and Wales in 1851, excluding scholars, wives and others engaged in household duties, 783,543 earned their living as domestic servants. [1] This represents a figure of more than one in five women so employed. By 1871, the proportion had risen to nearly one in three, as 1,225,014 out of 3,710,305 working women were employed in domestic service making it by far the largest occupation for women.

In thinking about the nineteenth century the picture that comes to mind is one of factories and mining. The fact that Britain's greatest industry in the Victorian period was not industrial is often overlooked. In 1900 domestic service continued to be the largest occupation in Edwardian Britain. [2] But despite its social and economic importance, until recently there has been a noticeable shortage of material on the subject. While other female occupations were investigated during the nineteenth century, domestic service was largely ignored. Historians

---

[1] L.F. Haimes, *In Their Place: Domestic Service in English Country Houses 1850-1870*, unpublished thesis, John Hopkins University, Baltimore, Maryland, (1981), p.25

[2] L. Lethbridge, *Servants: A Downstairs View of Twentieth-century Britain* (2013), p. 9

have also neglected the subject because matters of a 'domestic' nature concerning women were not regarded as being historically significant or worthy of serious academic consideration. Eric Richards noted in the 1970s that, 'economic historians have not felt justified in discussing the work of women as an analytically significant element in the process of economic growth in Britain.' [3] It is heartening to see more recently an increase in the number of books on the subject.

L. J. Williams and Dot Jones in their study of women's work in the nineteenth century show that domestic service dominated in England and Wales but the rate of participation in Wales was even higher. [4] From 1871 to 1901, domestic service accounted for over half the total number of women employed in Wales and the proportion in domestic service was ten per cent higher than in England.

The figures for Anglesey again confirm the dominance of domestic service as the largest employer of women. In 1871, one in every two working women on the island were domestic servants. The percentage of general domestic servants was higher in Anglesey than the average for England and Wales in 1851 and 1871. The percentage of housemaids was lower in Anglesey which suggests that the opportunities for more specialised employment opportunities were more limited than the national average.

Finding the evidence to support a local study of domestic servants is not an easy task. In this study, a wide range of source material was used but its value was often limited because there was no mention of women servants or because the records were too scanty to draw any firm conclusions. Other historians of women's history have made the point that that this field of enquiry poses great difficulties in terms of actual research and in seeking to

---

[3] E. Richards, 'Women in the British Economy Since About 1700: An Interpretation', History, 59, (1974), p.338

[4] L.J. Williams and D. Jones, 'Women and Work in Nineteenth Century Wales', Digest of Welsh Historical Statistics, L.J Williams (ed), (1985)

find explanations for the shortage of profitable source material. For these reasons, the discussion which follows is structured around general considerations about domestic service and local evidence is woven into this picture where it is available and appropriate.

Local studies have a value in their own right but they can also serve to enhance and sometimes call into question general theories that have been used and taken for granted as being correct. For example, the notion that the keeping or non-keeping of domestic servants is an indicator of class position in the nineteenth century has been a widely held view.

Seebohm Rowntree in his survey of York in 1899 took this criterion to establish the dividing line between 'the working classes and those of a higher social scale'. The Industrial Revolution that began in Britain roughly at the end of the 1700s provided new opportunities for wealth creation. An expanded middle class emerged and created the familiar images that we have of gender roles in the nineteenth century. In order to display their wealth, the middle classes tried to emulate the lifestyle of the landed aristocracy and employing servants was an essential ingredient in establishing their status. Even if all the paraphernalia of the very rich was out of reach, it was still possible to employ key servants.

Mrs Beeton's 'Book of Household Management' became a very popular publication during the nineteenth century. The biography by Kathryn Hughes in 2006, 'The Short Life and Long Times of Mrs Beeton' gives a fascinating account of the life of this young woman who became so well known and successful. When Mrs Beeton's book was first published in 1861, 60,000 copies were sold in the first year and this figure had increased to nearly 2 million by 1868. It was a big book with over a thousand pages and it provided advice on a vast range of household issues. Information was included about how many servants could be employed by households according to their income.

On an annual income of £1,000 a cook, a housemaid and perhaps a manservant could be employed whereas on an annual income of £200 only a young girl for rough work could be afforded. An income below £200 did not make one eligible for hiring servants at all according to Mrs Beeton.

The notion that servants were a necessary expression of middle class status, has led some historians to link the decline of domestic service in the late nineteenth century to the financial difficulties that this class faced at that time. However, in more recent years, historians have shown that this view is less cohesive than it was originally thought to be.

In addition to the lack of sources on domestic servants in the nineteenth century, it is difficult to distinguish between 'live in' servants and relatives of the family living in the household. The practice of employing young girls from within the family was very common. This occurred, for example, upon the death of a wife or mother, or the birth of children. In a society where household work was regarded as the woman's sphere of activity, the loss, incapacity or absence of a wife necessitated the recruitment of extra domestic help.

This calls into question Mrs Beeton's idea that it was impossible to employ a servant on an income less than two hundred pounds a year. Because of the extreme poverty of the nineteenth century, there was a ready supply of very cheap female labour, from the workhouse, the refuge, the industrial school or the prison. The Poor Law Guardians who were responsible for the poor in their parishes would be very keen to find places for young girls and there was a steady demand for servants from this source.

Another area that has received insufficient attention from historians is the influence of domestic service on migration. Domestic servants often travelled long distances from rural areas to take up positions in the cities. It is outside the scope of this book, but we know from oral testimony that many women from north Wales moved to

Liverpool, Manchester and London to work as servants. Many would have returned but equally, a large number would have remained or married in these locations. There was a high demand for servants which could not be met from the cities so that women and girls would find it relatively easy to find employment. In Liverpool, there are examples of Welsh speaking women who found employment with Welsh speaking families and would attend Welsh services in chapel and shop at the Welsh corner shop.

The importance of domestic service as a bridging occupation in the transition from rural to urban life has been underestimated as the focus of migration studies has centred on men moving to work in factories and mines. The historian McBride makes the point that 'domestic service was no longer simply a traditional occupation for rural - born individuals; it was also an active modernising agent which facilitated urban acculturation and occupational mobility in the urban environment.' [5]

Domestic service also sheds an interesting light on 'domestic ideology' in the nineteenth century. Ideas about what was regarded as 'acceptable' occupations for women were a key theme during the course of the century. Women and girls had always undertaken hard physical work and were employed in heavy industries like coal mining but as the century progressed it became less acceptable for them to be seen working alongside men in these harsh conditions. For example, legislation was put in place that excluded children and women from working underground.

A particular group of Christians, known as Evangelicals, were particularly influential in presenting images of the ideal woman. In the face of concerns prompted by the French Revolution and what seemed to them the dehumanising face of industrial development,

---

[5] T. McBride, The Domestic Service Revolution: The Modernisation of Household Service in England and France 1820-1920, (1976), p. 11

they promoted an image of women as 'angels in the home', protecting moral values and nurturing and educating children. Men inhabited separate spheres, men in the public and competitive world of work and commerce and women in the home creating a haven of peace and tranquility for the men to return to at the end of the day. According to this ideology, women were seen as superior to men as the 'gentler sex' with higher moral values and a non-aggressive attitude to life.

These ideas gained purchase and influenced many aspects of life and influenced attitudes towards women and work. In Wales, the role of women as the moral guardians of the nation was further highlighted in response to the report of the State of Education in Wales that was published in 1847. The report became known as the Treachery of the Blue Books (Brad y Llyfrau Gleision) because it presented a picture of the Welsh as a backward and ill-educated nation. Much of the blame was attributed to Welsh women and mothers who were seen as immoral, feckless and licentious.

In response to these criticisms of Welsh women attempts were made by writers and religious leaders to promote in Wales the ideas that had been presented by the Evangelicals earlier in the century in England. The non-conformist minister Evan Jones (Ieuan Gwynedd), for example, published a magazine called 'Y Gymraes' (The Welsh Woman) aimed at improving the moral values by giving advice to women housekeeping and for the education of their children. Eisteddfod essays also took up this theme and Welsh chapels supported the idealisation of women as perfect mothers and wives.

Employment opportunities narrowed for women as a result of domestic ideology. Legislation restricted or limited their hours in mines and factories and in one example from Anglesey it is apparent that women were much less inclined to work on the land because working alongside men in the fields was seen to be less acceptable. [6] As we have seen earlier from the employment figures, domestic service became the dominant occupation for women. It was hidden in the separate sphere of the home.

This raises an interesting dynamic about the relationship between mistresses and their servants. Mistresses themselves were restricted by domestic ideology but in the home, their control was absolute. However, the power and control their exercised in this domain, was at a cost to the other women they employed as their domestic servants.

The first part of this book looks at domestic servants in the homes of the landed gentry and aristocracy. This will demonstrate that employment in these settings was out of reach for most local women. Anglesey is well placed for a study of domestic servants in large country houses because a number of aristocratic families were resident on the island during the nineteenth century either in a permanent capacity or on a more seasonal basis. Land ownership on the island was concentrated in the hands of a small number of landowners. R. G. Thomas writing in the Transactions of the Anglesey Antiquarian Society estimates that twenty-three people owned 67% of the island in the mid eighteen thirties. [7] The estates also vary in size and reflect different capacities in financial terms of employing servants. Five estates have been selected to give examples of wage rates on the island. The records are not always complete or as detailed as one would like them to be but it is possible to compare wage rates in these establishments and make broader comparisons between rates in Anglesey and those in other areas of Britain. In addition, some interesting

---

[6] S.A. Williams, Unending Labour: Working Women in Nineteenth-Century Anglesey, Unpublished MPhil thesis (1990). I have published my academic work in the past using my full name – Sydna Ann Williams.

[7] R.G. Thomas, Anglesey County Politics, 1837-41, *Anglesey Antiquarian Society*, (1969-79), p.166

insights into master-servant relationships emerge in some of the records of the other Anglesey estates which will be dealt with in the course of the discussion.

The discussion on wage rates is based on the estate papers of Plas Newydd, Baron Hill, Gwredog, Henllys and Penrhos. The properties mentioned here can be seen on the map on page 6 that was produced in 1795 by John Evans and reproduced in 'Portraits of an Island – Eighteenth Century Anglesey', by Helen Ramage in 1987. The first of these estates, Plas Newydd in Llanedwen was the estate of the Earl of Uxbridge. In 1737, Sir Nicholas Bayly of Plas Newydd married Caroline, daughter and heiress of Lord Paget of Beaudesert, Staffordshire. Their second son and heir, Henry Bayly (1744-1812), took the name Paget upon succeeding to the barony of Beaudesert in 1769 and he was created Earl of Uxbridge in 1784. He consolidated the social and political status of the family in Anglesey and, together with Thomas Williams of Llanidan 1737-1802, formed the Mona Mine Company to work the rich deposits of copper in Parys Mountain. The estate was widespread and, in the mid thirties, consisted of 13,770 acres in forty parishes.

Baron Hill was larger again consisting of 17,086 acres across thirty six parishes. Samuel Hyatt was commissioned in 1776 to remodel Baron Hill, a Jacobean mansion situated in Beaumaris. The political power of the Bulkeley family of Baron Hill was enormous and Beaumaris represented a typical 'pocket borough' which gave the Bulkeleys the power to appoint one of their number or a person of their choosing to serve in Parliament. The historian E.A. Williams makes the point that, 'everything in Beaumaris depended on the Baron Hill family, for virtually the whole town, buildings and land, belonged to the estate.' [8]

---

[8]   E.A. Williams, *The Day Before Yesterday, Anglesey in the Nineteenth Century*, Translated by G. Wynne Griffith), (1988), p.26

The Penrhos estate was owned by John Stanley of Alderley, in Cheshire who married Maria Josepha Holroyd in 1798. The estate comprised 8,463 acres mainly situated in the north-west of the island. Henllys was one of the island's smaller estates with an estimated acreage of between 1,000 and 2,500 acres. Gwredog was one of the largest farms in Anglesey, the property of Mr Elias Jones who also owned a great of land in Penmaenmawr.

The smaller Anglesey properties have been included in order to provide a fair balance of estates in terms of size and political influence on the island. Only a minority of people were in a position to maintain large country houses and they provided work for only a small number of the local female population. It was noted earlier that the number of housemaids was lower in Anglesey than the national average which supports the view that opportunities were limited in this area of work on the island. The number of servants employed in each of these establishments would depend on the income level of the landowners and their personal preferences and needs.

Occasional references are also made to the Erddig estate in Wrexham. Six generations of the Yorke family lived at Erddig keeping up a tradition of painting and later photographing their servants and writing poems about them. Extensive research has been carried out by the National Trust on the life of the family and servants and, in addition, 'The Servants' Hall' by Merlin Waterson provides an excellent source on the history of the estate. [9]

---

[9] I am grateful to Jill Burton for conversations and information about Erddig based on the extensive research that she has carried out on the estate. Also, M. Waterson, *The Servants' Hall, A Domestic History of Erddig*, (1980)

These images of Baron Hill in Beaumaris and Penrhos in Holyhead in the nineteenth century (both demolished or in ruins now) show the wealth of these landed estates.

Baron Hill Mansion and Gardens
Courtesy of Anglesey Archives, Llangefni

Baron Hill Gardens
Courtesy of Anglesey Archives, Llangefni

Penrhos House and Gardens
*(I am very grateful to my friend J C Davies for these
images of Penrhos taken from his private collection)*

Servants in the Walled Garden at Penrhos
Courtesy of J C Davies, Holyhead

Chapter 2

The Landed Gentry and their Servants

Landowners were powerful figures in the nineteenth century and they could exert considerable influence over many aspects of social, economic and political affairs in the community. Power and influence was not restricted to one location either and it was possible to maintain two or more places of residence and to allocate time spent in each according to the demands of convention.

A typical pattern for the annual round was four months in London for the season followed by a month at Bath or some other spa, one month travelling and six months at the main country seat. The main activities which landlords might engage in while at their country houses were - dispensing and receiving hospitality, enjoying gardens and sport, supervising management of the estate and household, and participating in local affairs including the magistracy, churches and charities.

This lifestyle was maintained by the constant efforts, often behind the scenes, of domestic servants. These nineteenth century mansions contained within them two very separate worlds, one of ostentatious luxury for the leisured class and one of drudgery in much starker surroundings for the domestics. The layout of the buildings reflected the need to maintain a safe distance between the two. Jill Franklin, who looked at labour and planning in country houses stresses the importance which was placed on keeping the servants' wing or the working part of the house as invisible as possible. [1]

These service areas which could take up more than half the total ground area were situated in the basement or were hidden behind a screen of bushes. The study of house plans during the nineteenth century and the early twentieth century, according to Franklin, reveals many interesting points about changing attitudes towards the hiring of servants. In the early period the general practice in building houses was to establish the size of the service wing according to the maximum number of servants which could be afforded. The amount of work which was to be carried out by servants was therefore not seen to be of primary importance. Labour saving was not taken into account at all so that, for example, the kitchen was placed at a great distance away from the dining room to shield the family and guests from the nasty kitchen smells. This meant that the servants had to walk miles in a day to and from the service area to the dining room and the other rooms in the main block of the house.

The stairs also added to the distances which had to be covered by the servants. The buildings were planned in the knowledge that there existed an endless supply of cheap labour and this continued to be reflected in country house designs up to 1870. However, after this date a number of changes occurred which worked against the hiring of such large numbers of servants and this was reflected in the newer designs of country houses.

There were many subdivisions within country houses reflecting the layers of activities which took place within them. For example, the activities of children were separate

---

[1] J. Franklin, 'Troops of Servants: Labour and Planning in Country Houses 1840-1914', Victorian Studies, XIX, December, (1975), p. 211

from those of grown ups, as were those of men and women and often those of the family and their guests. In addition, there was the separation between the senior and junior staff. All these activities gave rise to a great deal of work for the servants because, apart from being available to deal with requests from their employers, a large number of rooms had to be kept clean and heated and oil lamps had to be cleaned, filled and trimmed.

In addition, because servants were so cheap to hire, labour saving devices tended not to be used. For example, central heating was possible and was used in some houses in the 1820s but, in general, open fires were preferred which meant that huge amounts of coal had to transported around the house and fireplaces had to cleaned daily. The number of meals which had to be served in different places in the house could sometimes run to ridiculous extremes.

As we have see in period dramas, domestic service in the homes of the upper classes was based on a highly segregated and hierarchical system. The duties of different servants within the household were clearly defined and each occupation was strictly placed within the overall power structure. Junior staff at the bottom of the hierarchy would, in some instances, have no contact whatsoever with their employers and only a limited acquaintance with the most senior staff. The division between low status and high status occupations was reflected in the whole organisation of work and it carried over into other areas such as practices at mealtimes when the senior staff would eat separately from the other servants. Movement up the hierarchy was possible through promotion and rights and privileges were passed on with the position. The historian Pamela Horn gives an example of a scullery maid who was upgraded to a kitchen maid which meant that the lady's maid could then say 'good morning' to her before the scullery-maid. [2]

---

[2] P. Horn, *The Rise and Fall of the Victorian Servant*, (1975), p. 49

Ranking in the female hierarchy was as follows:

Housekeeper
Lady's Maid
Governess
Cook
Nurse
Housemaids
Kitchen maids
Scullery maids
Laundry staff
* Occasional references are made to a 'between maid' or 'tweeny' (combined duties of housemaid and kitchen maid)

Housekeeper

According to the 1871 census there were 140,836 housekeepers in England and Wales; they formed around one-ninth of the total domestic workforce and were the next most numerous category to the general servant. Only a small number of these were employed in upper class households because the term covered a number of different sorts of occupations. In the country houses we are concerned with here the housekeeper was an important figure and the responsibilities attached to her job were considerable. Mrs Beetons' advice to the housekeeper was that, ' She must consider herself as the immediate representative of her mistress, and bring, to the management of the household, all those qualities of honesty, industry, and vigilance, in the same degree as if she were at the head of her own family. Constantly on the watch to detect any wrong-doing on the part of any of the domestics, she will overlook all that goes on in the house, and will see that every department is thoroughly attended to, and that the servants are comfortable, at the same time that their various duties are properly performed'. Mrs Beeton adds that she should be like 'Caesar's wife, 'above suspicion, and her honesty and sobriety unquestionable'. Pamela Horn points out that the large bunch of household keys she carried was a symbol of her authority and that, 'more than one subordinate learned to tremble on hearing the jangle of those keys as she walked along the corridor. As a sign of respect, she was referred to as 'Mrs' irrespective of her actual marital status.

According to Pamela Horn, the housekeeper was responsible for engaging and dismissing female servants and for supervising the housemaids, laundrymaids and still-room maids. She had to make sure that rooms were kept clean and made decisions on the arrangement of the bedrooms, including, in consultation with her mistress, which rooms to allocate to guests and their servants. She supervised the handling of the household linen and had control over the china closet and the stillroom department where cordials and preserves were made and stored. In this department she was assisted by the stillroom maid. She also had knowledge of first-aid so that she could 'distil healing waters' and make up medications like liquorice lozenges or scurvy-grass wine for invalids.

In addition to these duties she kept control over the household stores and kept the accounts. She also did some cooking, particularly the more intricate items such as confectionery, preserves, wines and pickles. The greater part of the needlework required in the house was also her responsibility. In some instances the housekeeper assisted her mistress in dispensing charity among the neighbouring poor and organising entertainments for the children of estate workers.

In being seen as the immediate representative of the mistress, the housekeeper's role was significant in filtering authority down from the employers to the junior staff and maintaining a system of deference. In class terms, the housekeeper had much more in common with the members of staff beneath her than with her employers but her position in the hierarchy separated her in important ways from her colleagues. Clearly, some housekeepers were shrewd in managing the boundaries between these two worlds. An example from Anglesey show just how clever the housekeeper could be in this mediating role.

In the Penrhos papers there is a collection of letters from the housekeeper, Elizabeth Sainsbury, to her mistress Lady Maria Stanley. There are two letters written in December 1816 and thirteen written at more or less weekly intervals between May 1st and 4th August 1819. [3]

It is clear that Elizabeth Sainsbury was well educated. She shows the required level of deference in her dealings with her mistress. It is striking, even from these few letters, that she played a central role in the organisation of the house and farm. As no evidence of this kind exists for the other Anglesey estates, it is difficult to judge how representative this was of housekeepers in general or whether this was an exceptional case.

Her husband was also employed on the estate and this may account for her involvement if, for example, she was the more capable of the two so that she took on more responsibility for the work on the estate. Some examples will give an idea of the range of her organisational abilities. She was involved in organising a school on the estate for eleven girls and fourteen boys and she bought material for them to make up into pinafores and shirts. She did the book keeping for the house and farm, including repairs. She sent detailed weekly lists of estate workers, how much they earned and what tasks they carried out. The accounts covered all outgoings including taxes and what cattle and sheep were bought and sold. She was involved in the purchasing of cattle. She was also informed about tenants and was active in looking after the poorer people in the community. In addition, she hired and discharged indoor

---

[3] P. Horn, *The Rise and Fall of the Victorian Servant*, (1975), p. 49

and outdoor staff. In the house, she supervised all the work
being done including the installation of water closets, the
decorating of rooms and the beds and bedding. She also
made wine, potted butter and preserved fruits such as
strawberries and cherries. She drew up inventories of
furniture and other items about the house and kept in regular
contact with her employers, sending chickens, pigeons,
lobsters, lamb and tongue to their London residence.

Elizabeth Sainsbury was extremely sharp and ingenious.
Underneath all the formality and deference in her manner,
it is clear that she knew how to get what she wanted from
her mistress. She was able to present her employers with a
view of themselves as charitable and caring individuals and
to use this to gain more from them.

These examples from her letters illustrate the point:

'The poor woman which I gave the blanket to last is dead
and has left four very small children, two boys and two
girls and one of them about a fortnight old, they are very
poor. Will your Ladyship allow me to give the two boys a
shirt each and the little girl a shift? I have given them a
shirt and cap for the little baby. I purchased from Martha
Owens 10 yards of cloth at 10d per yard and am having it
made up in the school for shirts and shifts.'

In another letter she says:

'The poor family are in great distress and I will do what I can
for them and I'm sure they feel themselves much obliged to
your Ladyship. I hope your Ladyship will not be angry at
what I am going to communicate, I found in the wine cellar
in the wall a bottle of wine which had been opened and as
the poor woman was so ill I divided it between her and
Hugh the Harper who was then very ill and since dead. I
would not have taken it for the want of myself but for the
wants of others. I did not consider it a crime.'

She also takes the side of the staff in a sympathetic manner and presents information to the mistress in a way that makes it quite clear what course of action should be taken. For example:

'I am sorry to inform your Ladyship that we have lost Bagshaw as he was to go off with the Packet to Liverpool yesterday and his family to their parish. He seemed very much hurt at leaving and wished me to ask your Ladyship if he should return again, if he should have his work. I told him he may make himself perfectly satisfied upon that point, I was sure it was your Ladyship's intention as long as he was able to work that he should be employed. I gave him 2/- upon your Ladyship's account. He shed tears and said he was very much obliged to your Ladyship and Sir John and the Young Ladies for every kindness he had ever had. He seemed to be very much afraid you would not let him return. Mr Price the overseer is gone with him.'

She takes up this matter again in another letter:

'In consequence of John Bagshaw being sent away the gardener has applied to me for another man in his place. I told him I could not put any other man in the garden until I had wrought (written) to your Ladyship. He seemed very much hurt and said it was out of the power of any three men to keep the gardens anything in order and if I may be allowed to give my opinion I do not think he possibly can keep them in order as I always find him and his men fully employed and never find them idle as I keep a very watchful eye upon them. Your Ladyship may appoint any of the labourers you think proper to go to the garden excepting John Davis but I should much rather the cowman as he is neither able nor willing to take care of the stock.'

In the next letter, which is a week later, the cowman is employed in the garden.

The last example shows how she used her position to benefit her own family. One of the rooms at Penrhos was being decorated and new curtains were bought so Elizabeth Sainsbury wondered if her mistress was thinking of buying a new carpet.

She says:

'Excuse me for taking the liberty of naming but should you be in want of any new carpeting, I have a near relation who would be glad to serve your Ladyship upon the lowest terms with the best Kidderminster carpeting - hope your Lady will not be displeased for my taking the liberty of naming him.'

Elizabeth Sainsbury was obviously a highly competent woman and she worked to the best of her ability to please her employer but at the same time she managed to gain benefits for others whenever it was possible to do so. She was extremely cost-conscious and there were several occasions when she tried to save money for her employer. For example, she was asked by her mistress to buy some linen but she says, 'the charge is so very high in this county, I think if your Ladyship would have the goodness to purchase it in Cheshire you could get it for a little more than half the money you could here.' [4]

It is unfortunate that only one side of the correspondence between Elizabeth Stanley and Lady Maria Stanley came to light in the course of this study. The lack of response from the the mistress is particularly disappointing when it comes to particular events such as

---

[4] Ibid., No 154

the discussion that took place about a servant named Betsy. She was first mentioned by Elizabeth Sainsbury on the 22 of May 1819. She wrote, 'the housemaid has been very ill this last two days, she has been unable to get up'. On the 28 of May, she wrote, 'the housemaid is better but she is still poorly'. The housemaid was 'still very poorly' on the 12 of June. On the 19th of June, Elizabeth Sainsbury wrote, 'in respect to Betsy's illness, she has now been regular for this last nine or ten weeks, sickness at the stomach, she has taken a remedy and likewise opening medicine twice from Mr Parry but has not been of any service to her. She is rather better this last two or three days she looks very ill and is very low in spirits.' [5]

On the 5th July, 1819, Elizabeth Sainsbury was clearly responding to Lady Stanley's suggestion that Betsy might be pregnant and replies saying:

'in respect to Betsy I was in the same opinion as your ladyship as she has every symptom of being a certain way. I have twice taken her to my room and told her if it was so not to conceal it from me. This day she likewise assured me that it is not so she still continues very poorly, it has given me a great deal of uneasiness about her but I hope she tells me the truth.' [6]

The references to Betsy did not continue and it is impossible to know what became of her.

In general, research carried out on the Erddig estate confirms the findings in this study that landowners did not tend to employ local women. The backgrounds of many of the servants on the estate have been traced and the majority in the nineteenth century were born outside the area. The housekeeper, Harriet Rogers, was an exception. The Rogers family were particularly loyal to the Yorke family and research undertaken by the National Trust suggests that nine members of the Rogers family worked on the estate – indoors and outdoors. The history is very interesting because the story began with Thomas Rogers (estate carpenter) being rescued from a press gang by Simon Yorke in 1815. Harriet was Thomas's youngest daughter who was born on the Erddig estate and began work there as a nursemaid. In the early 1820s she was promoted to lady's maid to Victoria Yorke and in this capacity accompanied her mistress on many journeys on the continent, visiting Paris, Vienna and many other cities all over Europe.

Harriet's family kept many of her Valentine cards showing that she rejected offers of marriage in favour of what the historian specialising in the life of the servants at Erddig has called a life as a 'career servant'. [7] She helped nurse the housekeeper Mary Webster until her death and then took up the position of housekeeper herself. She remained in this role as Cook/Housekeeper for nearly twenty years. She finally left Erddig to become a lady's maid to one of the Yorke sisters. It is interesting to note that 'Mrs Beeton' was included in the collection of books she took with her.

This is an unusual case in many respects because the records of her life from letters and diaries show that she was supported by the Yorke family in gaining an education and as lady's maid was given opportunities to travel. It is also very rare for a servant to be offered these chances for promotion.

Lady's Maid
Mrs Beeton in discussing the duties of the valet and the lady's maid says, 'they are placed near the persons of the master and mistress, receiving orders only from them, dressing them; accompanying them in all their journeys, the confidants and agents of their most unguarded moments, of their most secret habits.'

---

[7] See above Jill Burton

She goes on to say:

'deference to a master and mistress, and to their friends and visitors, is one of the implied terms of their engagement; and this deference must apply even to what may be considered their whims.'

The lady's maid was only employed in very wealthy households and her work experience was therefore very different from that of most domestic servants. The most obvious difference was that her work was less physically demanding. The lady's maid was also better educated than other domestic servants and she was likely to possess skills in dressmaking and other sorts of needlework. In addition, she was carefully selected according to her personality to fit the needs of the employer. Mrs Beeton stressed that the lady's maid should have a 'modest demeanour and a respectful reserve'.

The duties of the lady's maid in the household were entirely structured around the requirements of the mistress and included dressmaking, hairdressing, laundering special items of clothing, making up beauty lotions and generally caring for her mistress. This included the times when the mistress was ill. She also made sure that her mistress' room was clean and aired. The lady's maid was essentially available at all times to deal with the demands of her employer. This meant that her working day was very long and could include lonely periods of waiting around for her mistress to return from social events.

Lynne Haims found an excellent quote from an upper-class woman in 1822 that describes the work of the Lady's Maid:

'She **must not** have a will of her own in anything, & be always good-humoured & approve of everything her mistress likes. She **must not** have a great appetite or be the least of a **gourmand**, or gage when or how she dines, how often disturbed, or even if she has no dinner at all. She had better not drink anything but water.

She must **run quick** the instant she is **called** whatever she is about. Morning, noon and night she must not mind going without **sleep** if her mistress requires her attendance .... she **must** be a **first rate** vermin chaser.

She must be clean & sweet and very quick. She must have ears (strong ones), eyes & hands, but as for thinking in any way independent (if especially her mistress be a Whig of liberal **principles**) she must not think of such a thing ....

Implicit obedience the first essential; extraordinary dis-interestedness, united with a love of strict economy, the second. Honesty that will be the closest inspection; unceasing activity; unimpeachable good health & extreme good humour **indispensable requisites.'** [8]

In the larger households, such as Baron Hill and Plas Newydd two or three lady's maids were employed and this probably reduced their sense of isolation. For example, in 1818 there were three lady's maids in the employ of the Plas Newydd household, one for Lady Anglesey and two for the young ladies. [9]

There is a local reference to one lady's maid in 'Portrait of Jane Henrietta Adeane', a member of the Stanley family of Penrhos, Holyhead. Writing about her Aunt Ellin, Jane Adeane wrote of the newly appointed lady's maid saying:

'It must be very funny being Aunt Ellin's maid. She was given fair warning the first day, that Aunt Ellin would try and stand still the first two days while she was being dressed, but after that Aicheson must run after her about the room and catch her when she could. Aunt Ellin was afraid at first how she might take attending to Iser's toilette of a morning but she says she is very good and brings the

[8] L. Haimes, op cit., p. 216
[9] Bangor University, Plas Newydd Papers, VII, 3104

sponge for Iser's mouth and warms the towels all without any objection.' [10]

We can only assume that Iser was a dog.

Like the housekeeper, the lady's maid was in an interesting position in class terms; her position was the same as the other domestics in the household in that she received low wages for long hours of work but there was a certain amount of status attached to her occupation which put her above the rest. There are similarities between the lady's maid and the housekeeper in that they were both encouraged to identify themselves with the interests of the employer but the lady's maid was forced even further away from her colleagues because so much of her time was spent in the confines of the mistress's room.

The distance between them was often maintained by a mutual distrust. Pamela Horn makes the point that she was disliked because of her airs and graces and also because her closeness to the mistress of the house caused her to be suspected of tale bearing. She was also separated from the rest of the domestics because she was referred to as 'Miss '. The author of a pamphlet on the duties of the lady's maid drew attention to issue of class identification when s/he gave this advice:

'I trust you will bear constantly in mind that your elevation into comfort and luxury - your better clothes, your seat in the dressing-room and on your master's carriage, are only circumstances in your service, and not given you to last. Your heart should still be where your station is - among the poor.' [11]

Pamela Horn refers to the problems that confronted the lady's maid as she grew older. Mistresses preferred their

---

[10] Bangor University, Bangor MSS., 32169, 'Portrait of Jane Henrietta Adeane, by her niece, Violet Martineau, November 12, 1872
[11] P. Horn, op cit., p. 57

maids to be young so the plunge from luxury into unemployment could be sudden for an ageing maid. Once on the labour market, her qualifications were unsuitable for most other occupations in domestic service. For example, it was difficult for her to become a housekeeper or a cook because she lacked essential experience in the work. The lady's maid who did not marry could easily find herself therefore on the lower rung of the occupational ladder in her old age after experiencing some years in a more superior position.

Governess

The governess is further removed again from the main body of servants and strictly speaking should be excluded from the discussion but her role throws an interesting light on the ideology of the nineteenth century and the pressures on women to conform to the image of the 'angel in the home'. For women in the upper and middle classes this necessitated an appropriate education to enable them to hold an interesting conversation and display accomplishments such as playing the piano and discussing literature and poetry.

The governess, like the housekeeper and the lady's maid was placed in the higher ranks of the household staff but her class position was more clearly marked. In order to be considered suitable to teach the children of the wealthy classes it was necessary for the governess herself to be educated and sufficiently well bred to ensure that the children were taught correct etiquette.

The historian, M. J. Peterson in her discussion on the Victorian governess notes that there were contradictory definitions of the governess' role in society. She says, 'She was a lady, and therefore not a servant, but she was an employee, and therefore not of equal status with the wife and daughters of the house.' [12]

---

[12] M.J. Peterson, The Victorian Governess: Status Incongruence in Family and Society', Victorian Studies, 14, (1970-71), p. 10

The role of the governess received considerable attention during the nineteenth century probably as a result of her contradictory class position. Her role set her outside the ideal of the Victorian middle class woman because she was a worker. Ideally, middle class women should not need to work but if they did, how were they to be treated? This uncertainty about her class position would influence all her relationships with other staff and indeed, her employers.

The ability to teach French and Music was important for the governess. Sir John Thomas Stanley wrote to his mother, Lady Margaret Stanley, in February 1807 saying that a new governess had been appointed in the Stanley household who, he said 'promises well but we discover knows very little of French'. [13] In fact, she only stayed until July the same year when she was replaced by another governess who was hired for the Stanleys in London by a woman called Louisa Chinton. It is not clear whether Louisa Chinton was from an agency or whether she was a family friend or employee.

The new governess was described as being twenty years of age, decently connected, of good appearance with pleasing manners and a sensible way of speaking. Reading between the lines, one gets the impression that the Stanleys were a bit disappointed with her because they would have preferred a French governess. There was a certain degree of distinction associated with having a French governess at this time. The new governess was in fact English but she could 'speak French as well as a foreigner'. Their disappointment was compounded because she did not possess the necessary skills in teaching music and Lady Stanley expressed her disappointment saying:

---

[13] Penrhos Papers 2, No 392

'She knows nothing of music, and as the world will have ladies to play some little on the harpsichord, is a serious deficiency and will throw us into a considerable expense in getting a master.' [14]

The salary of the governess in question was more than halved because of these shortcomings. She was given £30 a year because governesses with musical skills were asking for between £60 and £100 a year. The Stanleys failed on two occasions to find a suitable governess which suggests there was a shortage of candidates with the necessary skills for the job in such upper class households.

A letter found in the Amlwch papers supports the view that governesses with appropriate qualifications were difficult to find. Writing to her friend in 1840, a governess says:

'I have at last met with a very eligible situation as governess with a pious family of the name of Lloyd. They are of our connection, Mr Lloyd is an elder. I am paid £30 per annum. I should have gone to Mrs Jones of Machynlleth but I am not able to teach French, music or drawing.' [15]

The letter suggests that this governess was working to support her sisters on the death of their mother. She says:

'At times I am ready to break my heart after my dear motherless sisters and my mind wanders to Llangefni Church yard where rests my fond mother, two affectionate brothers and many a dear friend.' [16]

It is likely that a number of women were faced with similar obstacles in trying to find a position as governess because

---

[14] Ibid., No 395
[15] Bangor University, Amlwch Papers 3, 21
[16] Ibid.

they possessed only limited skills for the kind of work that was on offer. Situations in wealthy country houses were therefore out of the question for most of them because their own education was not adequate for the demands of the job.

Religious considerations were also important for both employers and employees. In the letter from the governess mentioned above, the writer referred to the Chapel in Betws y Coed, saying that the building was small but the 'society' was very large. The Chapel provided a common space that was shared by employers and employees.

Cook

The cook ranked second in the domestic hierarchy next to the housekeeper. According to Mrs Beeton she was the 'queen of the kitchen' and, depending on the size of the household, was in charge of a number of kitchen maids and scullery-maids. The cook was an important figure in the household as the demands on the kitchen could be great, given the amount of catering undertaken for the family and guests. Entertaining was a central feature in large households providing an opportunity for the rich to display their wealth. Good food presented in an elaborate fashion was crucial to the success of these events.

Mrs Beeton's 'Book of Household Management' gives numerous examples of highly decorated items of food that cooks were expected to prepare. This work was highly skilled and many hours of preparation and cooking went into some of these dishes. The 'Servant's Practical Guide' stated that, 'some ladies stand very much in awe of their cooks, knowing that those who consider themselves to be thoroughly experienced will not brook fault finding, or interference with their manner of cooking, and give notice to leave on the smallest pretext. Thus when ladies obtain a really good cook, they deal with her delicately, and are inclined to let her have her own way with regard to serving the dinner.'

The work in the kitchen was extremely hard and there was a relentless regularity to the tasks performed by the cook consisting of preparation, cooking, serving and clearing up. This process was repeated three or four times in a day. Kitchens were badly ventilated so that at the peak of the cooking stage, the heat could be punishingly hot and steamy. The kitchen was dominated by a stove that was described by one writer as 'a dirty, inefficient, labour making, fuel devouring monster that made the place unbearable in the summer'. Gas ovens would have been much cleaner and less labour intensive, but the use of gas in domestic appliances was slow in gaining ground.

Depending on how the division of labour was organised between the cook and the housekeeper, the cook could deal with the tradesmen when they delivered goods to the kitchen. In this role, she could receive 'perks'. Taken to an extreme, the cook could run a fairly profitable business in negotiating 'commissions' or 'kickbacks' with the shopkeeper. In large households there were cases where the cook would sell back some of the provisions to the shopkeeper for her own profit by cutting down on the amount of food given to the rest of the servants. This practice could only be carried out in a household where the housekeeper was less than efficient.

It was common for the cook have certain perquisites written in to her contract. This meant that she had the right to sell leftover items, such as, dripping, ashes, rabbit skins and old tea leaves. Like the housekeeper, the cook was in a relatively secure position if she satisfied the needs of the employer. Old age and illness were of course factors which gave rise to uncertainty but compared to the lady's maid, the cook was much better off. If she had no dependants, she could save her wages and 'perks'. She did not have expensive outgoings for clothes as did the governess, for example.

The majority of cooks were female but in some

establishments it was fashionable to employ a male, particularly if he was French. Lynne Haims, in her sample of country houses found that 10 out of 12 cooks in 1851 were female and that in 1861 the figure was 12 out of 18. The male cooks tended to be foreign born. [17]

From the available evidence, the only two estates on Anglesey to employ male cooks were Baron Hill and Plas Newydd. There is a reference in 1886 in the Baron Hill accounts to a cook named Gaillard who was almost certainly male because of the high wages he received. At Plas Newydd a cook named Mr Holinix was employed and he too received substantially higher wages than the average received by female cook. [18]

Jane Adeane of Penrhos referred to a male cook when she gave an account of a luncheon which was arranged for the Prince of Wales in 1873. She wrote of the event, 'The luncheon for the Prince of Wales (laying foundation stone of Breakwater) and 24 others was prepared in the dining room. The rest had a stand up luncheon in the servant's hall, to which the passage had been made beautiful with flowers. The Cook turned out to be a friend and gave Aunt Ellin great trouble. I think I told you how he overheated the kitchen chimney and it caught fire and a great many dishes were spoilt and had to be done over again, and yesterday he turned spiteful and made a great bother so that they were glad to get him out of the house.' [19]

Nursemaid

The head nurse was a central figure in the homes of the wealthy. She was chosen with the same care as the governess. Mrs Beeton described the qualities of the head nurse in this way, 'patience and good temper are

---

[17] L. Haims, op. cit., p.227
[18] Plas Newydd, VII, 3104
[19] Bangor MSS., 32169, August 20 1873

indispensable; truthfulness, purity of manners, minute attention to cleanliness, and docility and obedience are almost essential.'

The Stanleys of Penrhos in 1807 were looking for a new nurse and Sir John Thomas Stanley wrote to his mother describing the kind of woman they were seeking to hire. He wrote, 'we shall want a decent behaved young woman to attend to the nurseries. We thought there would be a advantage in hiring a foreigner to talk French with the children. Do you think you can find one for us? We want humility, manners and morals. We are not very anxious about the kind of religion provided it is Religion and not Bigotry. It would not do for the children to be told they will be damned if not Roman Catholics but we are not averse to their supposing that a Roman Catholick may go to heaven.' [20]

The ability to speak French was again stressed as being an advantage. Religion was also seen to be important and it is possible that other employers were even less tolerant of Roman Catholics than the Stanleys.

The nursery was run as a separate department within the household and the children and their nurses ate meals in the nursery. Pamela Horn outlines the demarcation disputes which arose as a result of this separation, for example, to do with fetching and carrying. There could be conflicts too between the cook and the head nurse about special food for the children. The head nurse could be viewed as an unpopular figure by the rest of the household staff because of her remoteness and the superiority of her position that gave rise to additional demands on the other domestics.

The duties of the head nurse covered all aspects of child care like washing, dressing and feeding the children but also caring for their emotional well-being. It is an interesting feature of the nineteenth century that the

---

[20] Penrhos, 2, 392

wealthy handed over responsibility to such staff for disciplining children and giving them their moral values. Wealthy Victorian parents involved in their own worlds might only see their children for short periods and nurses were therefore to a great degree responsible for how children would turn out. The extent to which parents participated in the rearing of their children would vary enormously but it is still the case that nurses were influential figures in the lives of the children who were reared by them.

The head nurse was assisted by the under-nursemaid or nursemaids. The duties of the under-nursemaid according to Mrs Beeton were as follows:

'The under nursemaid lights the fires, sweeps, scours, and dusts the rooms, and makes the beds, empties the slops and carries up water, brings up and removes the nursery meals, washes and dresses all the children, except the infant, and assists in mending.'

Jane Adeane of Penrhos wrote an account of a tragic accident that happened in Holyhead involving nursemaids and their charges. The account of the incident that took place in 1817 is very revealing and is therefore told as it was written by Jane Adeane.

'Emmy and Elfida were taken to bathe off the rocks by their nurse, accompanied by two of the housemaids. The nurse had been strictly forbidden to let the children bathe anywhere but the regular bathing place; however it was a very hot day and she thought it would be easier to go to the rocks which were much nearer. The two maids went into the sea, dipped Emmy, and gave her back to the nurse to be dressed; then Elfrida was dipped twice. She wanted to come out, but the nurse said she must be dipped again, the poor child, who was barely four years old, begged not, but in vain. The maids were in the act of dipping her, when a great wave came and washed them all off their feet as they stood on the slippery seaweed. The nurse screamed and rushed into the water after Elfrida, calling to Emmy to run for help. Poor little Emmy was only 8 years old, she was still in her little white shift, and terrified at seeing her younger sister swept away. However she started to run home across the park, and soon met the coachman exercising some of the horses. He, seeing her dressed only in her shift, thought the nurse had let her run about undressed on account of the heat, and discreetly rode away. Poor Emmy ran on, but next met some of the black Welsh cattle, which alarmed her still more, so that she made a circuit instead of running straight to the house. When she did reach it she rushed to the schoolroom and threw herself upon the governess, exclaiming "Oh come! Oh come! Elfrida is drowned!" The governess scarcely believed her ears, but she roused the household and hastened to the spot, only to find that Elfrida and the 3 maids had been carried away beyond hope of rescue. Truly the shock and terror of the accident would have been enough to unbalance poor Emmy's brain, but the saddest part was that Lady Maria could never forgive her for not being the one drowned. Elfrida had been her youngest and favourite child. Her mother also always believed that Emmy might have reached the house in time for help to be bought, if she had not turned aside to avoid the cattle.' [21]

The nurse clearly had not obeyed the instructions given to her. The parents were out riding that day so she and the housemaids had taken a risk by bathing nearer to the house thinking that they would not be found out. It is interesting that Jane Adeane's account of the incident, while stating that the nurse had been disobedient, did not unduly place

---

[21] Bangor MSS., 32169, pp. 205-206

the blame for the incident on her. The fact that the coachman did not consider it good manners to respond to Emmy shows the enormity of the divide between the family and the servants and the need at all times for servants to be 'invisible'.

Housemaids

A number of housemaids were employed in the households in the homes of the aristocracy, and a clear hierarchy existed. The head maid carried out the lighter tasks and supervised the work of the under housemaids. Each maid was given a set of specific tasks so that, for example, one housemaid would work entirely for her fellow servants, another would be employed in the schoolroom, and others performed general duties.

In Plas Newydd in 1818, one housemaid was described as 'The Young Ladies Housemaid'. [22] There would also be parlour maids and chambermaids. The duties of the under housemaids were numerous and as with all occupations within domestic service there was a grinding monotony attached to duties that had to be performed. Lynne Haims on the basis of the information she found in a household employing three housemaids, identifies their main duties as follows:

'After rising at 5:00 a.m. daily (4:30 a.m. on cleaning days), the upper housemaid was to dust the drawing room and sweep it, and dust and sweep with tea leaves the dining room, library, and smoking room; the third housemaid was to clean the grates in these last three rooms, dust and sweep the school room and entrance hall steps, and clean all the brass. Meanwhile, the upper housemaid was attending to the hot water and fires for master, mistress, and visitors, while the second housemaid did the same for

[22] Plas Newydd, VII, 3104

children and governesses. Only after all this was completed were the housemaids supposed to eat their breakfast.' [23]

Because servants were supposed to be 'invisible', much of their work had to be completed before the family came downstairs in the morning. Remaining 'behind the scenes', they cleaned the bedrooms while the family were at breakfast. This included emptying the slops and carrying out a methodical series of cleaning and dusting operations. Mrs Beeton gave an outline of the steps involved which included, firstly, moving velvet chairs and other things injured by dust into another room then covering the remaining surfaces to protect them from dust. Secondly, the feather mattress was 'shaken, beaten, taken up and opened several times, so as thoroughly to separate the feathers'. Feather mattresses were notoriously bad for making dust and for harbouring vermin. Thirdly, the bed was made up and finally, the carpet was swept and the room was dusted. This process was repeated in all the bedrooms.

At Penrhyn Castle all the housemaids were dressed identically in black aprons and white lace caps. They were even recruited to match each other in height. Housemaids were not allowed to be in the front part of the castle after 9am and all servants had to use the Secondary Staircase, next to Grand Stairs so that staff did not meet family and guests. [24]

The pace of their work did not slacken as the day wore on because they had other tasks to perform, such as, cleaning the grates, filling the coal boxes, cleaning the steps, cleaning other rooms in the house, carrying water to and from the bedrooms and responding to the on-going demands of their employers.

---

[23] L. Haimes, op. cit., p.207
[24] S. Evans, *Life Below Stairs in the Victorian and Edwardian Country House*, National Trust, (2011), p. 155

In addition to these daily tasks there were weekly cleaning days when a particular section of the house was given a more thorough clean and spring cleaning sessions when bigger jobs were undertaken such as taking up and beating the carpets. Inventions and the application of new principles that could have lightened this load were slow in coming. Bathrooms were not a common feature in the households of the early Victorian period. The 'hopper' water closet was invented in the 1790s but it took until 1889 before the washdown closet was invented. One of the ongoing duties of the housemaid was therefore the emptying of slop buckets and these had to be carried away discretely. These tasks performed by the housemaid were further hampered by the fact that running water did not reach the upstairs of houses until the 1870s. The housemaid therefore had to carry water from the basement to the upper rooms of the house for her own cleaning needs and for the family's ablutions. On average clean water had to be replaced four times a day for each person the housemaid served. Until the water supply reached upstairs hot water for baths also had to be carried up many flights of stairs.

A book in written by 'A Lady' in 1850 called 'Commonsense for Housemaids' identified the enemies of the housemaid as, 'dust, soot, smoke, insects of various kinds and bad smells innumerable'. [25]

Gas was not very popular for domestic use either for heating or lighting so housemaids continued to carry out these tedious and time consuming tasks around the house. Apart from constantly having to see to the fires in the house there was the additional work of coping with dust and soot on surfaces, furniture and drapes. The blackleading of grates was a major occupation for the

---

[25] S.J. Richardson, 'The Servant Question: A Study of the Domestic Labour Market 1851-1911', MPhil., (University of London 1967), p.59

housemaid. Coal was cheap as was domestic labour and while this continued to be the case there was little impetus for change. The Victorian obsession with clutter and elaborate furnishings also added to the work of the housemaid. The furniture was heavy and ornately carved and there were numerous wall hangings and pictures. There were also umpteen ornaments in glass, china and silver and carved, gilt framed mirrors.

Labour saving devices did exist but employers lacked the incentive to invest in them. For example, the 'Ukanusa Drudgee' (a mop and bucket) had long been available but servants continued to have to get down on their hands and knees to scrub floors. Also, the daily ritual of scrubbing stone doorsteps could have been made easier by the adoption of other materials such as brickwork, bronze and Doulton. It took until the late 1870s for brass fingerplates, door knockers and letter boxes to be replaced by cast iron that was much easier to clean.

The cleaning materials and polishes used by housemaids also had to be made on the premises. Mrs Beeton gives a number of recipes for substances to polish grates, remove bad smells, clean marble, brighten gilt frames, make paste for paper hanging, killing crickets and beetles and so on.

Kitchen maids and Scullery maids

According to Mrs Beeton the duties of kitchen maids and scullery maid were almost identical; they assisted the cook and kept the scullery and kitchen utensils clean. However, the kitchen maids did the more important work while scullery maids did the coarser work in the kitchen. This meant that the more senior kitchen maids attended to the cooking of staff meals and the cook concentrated on the meals for 'upstairs'. They also carried out the more laborious tasks such as chopping while the cook did the more intricate jobs. The vegetables were prepared by the more junior kitchen maids depending on the number of servants employed. Scullery maids washed the pots and pans and scrubbed floors and surfaces. They were also the first up in the morning to light the kitchen fire, clean the kitchen and steps, and lay the table for the servants' breakfast.

Reference has already been made to the conditions in the kitchen such as the changes of temperature and the need to constantly re-fuel the stove. The work was very strenuous because the pots and pans were large and heavy to carry around when full of food. Also, the scullery maids had to stoop for long periods over the sink to wash the dirty pots and when large numbers of people were being catered for, the work was absolutely crushing.

The reluctance of employers to adopt labour saving devices again impacted on the tasks performed by kitchen maids. Kitchen utensils were commonly made of copper and these had to be kept clean and polished. The wooden tables in the kitchen also had to be scrubbed white and the floors cleaned on hands and knees.

In terms of status, kitchen maids and scullery maids were at the bottom of the domestic hierarchy. This meant that they were directly under the supervision of the upper servants and they also served as 'servants' to them. One former servant described this process, 'there is a lot of one servant waiting on another, the under ones of each department doing it, they in turn being waited on, when promoted'. [26]

The food they ate was also different on occasions to that eaten by the senior servants. One former servant described the procedure at mealtimes in one establishment in this way, 'Old rules were kept up, we were not allowed to converse at the servants' hall dinner, until the "quality" usually called "Pugs" had left the hall, consisting of

[26] L. Haimes, op. cit., p. 209

housekeeper, cook, lady's maid, valets, butler, formed quite a procession to the steward's room, where they had .....well, we were not supposed to know what they had'. [27]

Because of their position at the lower end of the servant hierarchy, they would have very little contact with the employers.

This quote from Annie Evans, a scullery maid at Penrhyn Castle, describes the situation in 1908:

'We were not allowed to speak directly with Lady Penrhyn, who dealt only through the housekeeper or cook. Cook used to go to her room every morning after prayers to discuss the day's meals and get her orders. We never really knew how the gentry lived, and so were quite content'. [28]

The sleeping quarters of the lower servants were also much worse than those of the senior servants. The housekeeper, for example, would have her own bedroom and a sitting room which was likely to be very comfortable and well furnished. The lower servants however shared rooms and they lacked space for privacy and relaxation. This would inevitably lead to tensions at times.

Laundry maids

The washing machine was not invented until about 1885 and so the laundry was a necessary feature of the Victorian country house. The work in the laundry was organised on a weekly basis and consisted of a series of separate operations, namely, washing, drying and ironing. Pamela Horn outlines the main duties of the laundry maid as firstly, entering into her washing-book the articles of clothing committed to her care. Secondly, the items had to

---

[27] Ibid., p.223
[28] S. Evans, op cit., p.17

be separated into various piles according to colour and material. Thirdly, the actual washing and rinsing would take at least three days depending on the size of the household. A former laundry maid in one household recalled how she and two others washed a thousand table napkins each week along with other items. Finally, the items were mangled, starched and ironed.

Conditions in the laundry, like the kitchen, went through dramatic changes in temperature according to the various stages in the process of washing. During the peak of the process the heat could be unbearably hot and steamy. It is likely that such extremes of temperature had a detrimental effect on the health of the women who worked in these areas.

The physical strain attached to the job was enormous. The work entailed spending many hours stooping over the washing tub. It also demanded great strength to deal with the weight of some of the items especially when they were wet. As with cooking, the job relied on the operation of basic scientific principles. Although the knowledge of these principles was not formally understood by domestic staff, the application of them was often complicated.

For example, Mrs Beeton gave this advice to the laundry maid in relation to the use of soda: ' Coloured muslins, cottons, and linens require a milder treatment; any application of soda will discharge the colour, and soaking all night, even in pure water, deteriorates the more delicate tints. When ready for washing, if not too dirty, they should be put into cold water and washed very speedily, using common yellow soap, which should be rinsed off immediately. When washed thoroughly they should be rinsed in succession, in soft water, in which common salt has been dissolved, in the proportion of a handful to three or four gallons.'

Disasters could easily occur if the laundry maid did not understand the materials she was dealing with and their effects on different sorts of fabric. Stain removal was also a complicated process which entailed using the correct chemical to tackle the particular stain without damaging the fabric. Ironing too demanded an understanding of the effect of heat on different sorts of fabric and the temperature had to be regulated when all the laundry maid had was an iron and the fire. The responsibility was great for the laundry maid who had to treat the valued items of clothing which belonged to her employers or their guests.

Chapter 3

Wages and Conditions of Service

Wage rates for domestic servants are very difficult to establish because factors other than 'money wages' have to be taken into account. There are also a number of variables such as location and the size of the establishment which have to be considered. Wages in London were higher than those in other parts of the country and rates in larger establishments tended to be higher than those in smaller households. The historian John Burnett has made the point that large establishments formed their own economic systems which to some degree protected them from market forces. [1] The existence of wage differentials created a system which was self-enclosed and which gave the staff the illusion if not the reality that it was possible to rise through the ranks. Also, status and the privileges attached to particular occupations were important factors in addition to 'money wages' and they contributed to the overall value of the job.

There is a shortage of systematic information about the wages of servants because they were not the subject of any government enquiries until the end of the nineteenth century. What information we do have is drawn from a variety

---

[1] J. Burnett, *Useful Toil, Autobiographies of Working people From the 1820s to the 1920s*, (1974), p. 158

of sources including household manuals, general wage patterns drawn up by other historians and specific studies on domestic servants. The first source is the least reliable because it is questionable that employers actually adhered to the advice which was given to them in these books. The second source is useful but it sometimes lacks sufficient detail because it does not deal specifically with domestic servants. The third source is more valuable but because there are so few studies on domestic service, it is difficult to build up a picture of regional differences in wage levels.

However a combination of these sources will give an approximate idea of national wage rates so that local figures can be seen in a broader context. There is one major problem with the local figures in that they do not run continuously over a given period. The figures we have are only available for isolated years and they do not run in a systematic manner. It is impossible to get a match between national figures which are themselves scanty and local figures which are even more sparse. Comparisons as such are therefore out of the question and the most that can be achieved is a rough estimate of differences or similarities.

The other point, following on from the earlier discussion, is that we are dealing mainly with money paid out in cash for wages. There are other considerations such as board and lodging which have a bearing on the amount paid.

The term guinea is used in the figures below and this refers to a value of one pound and one shilling (21 shillings). Mrs Beeton set out the following as average annual wages in 1861.

'Servants – everything found or an allowance for the same

Housekeeper	From	£30 - £60
Lady's Maid		£25 - £40
Cook		£20 - £60
Kitchen Maid		£16 - £28
Scullery Maid		£14 - £18
Head Nurse		£25 - £35

Under Nurse	£12 - £18
Head Laundry Maid	£22 - £30
Under Laundry Maid	£12 - £20
Parlour Maid	£20 - £35
Head Housemaid	£20 - £28
Under Housemaid	£14 - £18
General Servant	£12 - £28

Figures taken from Pamela Horn, Lynne Haimes and the Board of Trade have been used as a basis for comparison. Annual wages of domestic servants employed at Milton Manor, Berkshire, (taken from Pamela Horn, the Rise and Fall of the Victorian Domestic Servant) and Annual Wages of Domestic Servants (taken from Lynne Haims: In Their Place: Domestic Service in English Country Houses 1850-1870).

Pamela Horn, Milton Manor, Berkshire

	1845	1850
Housekeeper	£25	£20
Lady's maid	£16	£16
Cook	£11	£13
Housemaid	£12	£11

Lynne Haimes

	Average	Range
Housekeeper	20-63	37.3
Lady's Maid	10-31.5	20.2
Head Nurse	26.3-31.5	28.6
Cook (female)	20-30	25.0
Upper housemaid	16-18.9	17.5
Upper laundrymaid	13-21	18.0
Under housemaid	8-16.8	12.1
Stillroom maid	5-18.9	12.7
Nursemaid	4.5-10	7.3
Under laundrymaid	10-16.8	13.3

| Kitchenmaid | 8.4-30 | 18.0 |
| Scullerymaid | 8.4-14.7 | 11.2 |

Figures below are taken from the Board of Trade in the 1890s based on actual returns from 2,000 households. (The National Archives)

Class of Work	Age	Average Annual Wage
Between maid	19	£10.7
Scullery maid	19	£13
Kitchen maid	20	£15
Nurse-housemaid	21-25	£16
General domestic	21-25	£14.6
Housemaid	21-25	£16.2
Nurse	25-30	£20.1
Parlour maid	25-30	£20.6
Laundry maid	25-30	£23.6
Cook	25-30	£20.2
Lady's maid	30-35	£24.7
Cook-housekeeper	40	£35.6
Housekeeper	40	£52.5

The local figures are sparse by comparison. Examples from Erddig and Penrhyn Castle have been added to the Anglesey figures where possible. Distinctions between upper and lower servants are not usually noted in the account books; they are listed under the general headings like 'housemaids' or 'kitchen maids'. When this is not the case, the relevant information is given. Wherever possible board wages have been excluded.

Housekeeper

	Year	Wages
Penrhos	1799	30 gns + tea
	1854	£30.00.
Plas Newydd	1804	£36.15.0

	1816	40 gns
Erddig	1874	£35.0.0
Penrhyn Castle	1883	£50
Lady's Maid		
Baron Hill	1803	12gns
Plas Newydd	1816	20gns
Henllys	1832	£9.0.0
	1839	£10.0.0
Cook		
Plas Newydd – male cook	1816	120gns
Henllys	1830	£14.0.0
	1832	£13.0.0
	1836	£14.0.0
	1842	£14.0.0
Baron Hill – male cook	1886	£238.00.
Penrhyn Castle – male cook	1883	£150
Nurse		
Plas Newydd	1816	22gns
Junior Nurse	1816	12gns
Gwredog	1862	£7.0.0.
	1868	£9.0.0.
	1870	£10.0.0.
	1873	£10.0.0.
Housemaids		
Plas Newydd	1804	8gns
	1815	12gns
	1832	12gns
Baron Hill	1801	7gns
	1841	12gns
Gwredog	1886	£12.0.0.
	1899	£14.0.0.
Henllys	1836	£8.0.0.
	1841	£10.0.0.
Penrhos	1832	10gns
	1853	£12.0.0.
	1854	£14.0.0.

Erddig	1805	£10.10.0.
	1814	£12.0.0.
	1874	£17.0.0.
Scullery maids		
Plas Newydd	1816	12gns
Baron Hill	1846	8gns
Penrhos	1819	8gns
Erddig	1874	£6.10.0.
	1877	£10.0.0.
Penrhyn Castle (kitchenmaids)	1883	£12-£24
Laundry maids		
Plas Newydd	1816	16gns
Baron Hill	1832	10gns
Gwredog	1853	£12.0.0.

* On the basis of a Retail Price Index conversion to today's approximate values (using Measuring Worth) the difference between males and females is noteworthy. For example, the figure for the male cook at Plas Newydd is £8,610; the male cook at Baron Hill is £23,000 and the female cook at Henllys is £1,120. On the same basis figures from the Board of Trade above for cooks at £20.2 is £1,990 and the housekeeper at £52.5 is £5,160 in approximate present day value.

The fit between national and local wage rates is surprisingly close considering the general paucity of evidence. The wage rates of lower grade servants in Anglesey were slightly lower in Anglesey than those found by Haimes. The differential between male and female cooks is noticeable and employers were clearly prepared to pay for the higher status that was associated with male cooks. Rates in Mrs Beeton's Book of Household Management were noticeably higher than the examples from the servant-employing households noted here. Employers did not necessarily follow the advice given to them in such literature.

A document from the Plas Newydd papers gives a full list of all the staff employed in 1816 and it demonstrates clearly the different levels in the servant hierarchy and the differences between the wages paid to men and women.[2] Apart from the senior female roles, all the male servants are paid more than women staff. It is noteworthy too for the dearth of Welsh names.

Servants Wages in the Quarter Ending Sept 30th 1816 – guineas per annum

Jane Goodman (Housekeeper)	40
Ann Collins (Nurse)	20
Elizabeth Blackford (Lady Anglesey's Maid)	20
Mary Baldwin (Young Ladies Maid)	20
Elizabeth Bevans (Young Ladies Maid)	14
Charlotte Beaumont (Young Ladies Maid)	12
Elizabeth Coindett (Nursery Maid)	12
Mary Reament (Housemaid)	15
Sarah Peters (Housemaid)	12
Esther Roper (Housemaid)	12
Sarah Hammond (Stillroom Maid)	12
Mary Garrett (Laundry Maid)	20
Jane Hodgson (Laundry Maid)	16
Mary Cronk (Laundry Maid)	12
Elizabeth Jones (Laundry Maid)	12
Martha Painter (Kitchenmaid)	20
Hannah Woolmer (Scullery Maid)	12
John Page (Housesteward)	100
George Wakeley (Groom of the Chamber)	60
Mathew White (Valet)	45
Nicholas Molinix (Cook)	120
George Gill (Porter)	30
John Wetton (Footman)	25
Joseph West (Footman)	25

---

[2] Bangor University, Plas Newydd MSS

Edward Johnson (Footman and Baker)	25
Thomas Turner (Young Ladies Foorman)	25
Bruster Everett (Under Butler)	25
Williams Woolmer (Stewards Room Boy)	16

More than in any other occupation, workers in domestic service relied on non-monetary benefits to improve their general standard of living. The most important of these was food and accommodation, the quality of which could vary considerably from one place to another. It is difficult to give a monetary value to these sorts of provisions because they have to be seen in the general context of servant-employer relations. The quality of the provisions supplied by the employer was likely to reflect his or her general attitude towards the servant class. It is impossible to set a standard which takes account of all the factors which had an influence on the quality of life of servants.

An approximate estimate of what employers considered to be suitable living standards for servants can be found by looking at board wages. These were payments paid in cash to servants when the employers were away which were supposed to cover the cost of meals. The owners of the larger estates on Anglesey spent some time away from their residences and it has been possible to find some examples of the sums paid.

For example:
Penrhos 1859 Housemaids were paid 8s. a week board wages.
Plas Newydd 1820 Housemaids were paid between 8s. and 10s. a week board wages.
Baron Hill 1832 senior staff were paid 16s. a week board wages while housemaids, laundry maids and kitchen maids were paid between 8s. and 10s. a week board wages.

As would be expected, senior staff were generally paid more than junior staff and, as is shown in the Baron Hill example, the difference could be quite substantial with the senior staff receiving almost double the amount given to the junior staff. As other writers on the subject have pointed out, it was the junior staff who were most in need of food because they were likely to be young workers who had to undertake the most arduous tasks in the household.

In addition to board wages, allowances were often given to servants for beer or tea and sugar. Written examples of allowances being given for tea are limited in the local records and it is likely that most of these agreements were made verbally. Commodities such as tea and sugar were expensive during the first half of the nineteenth century and allowances for these items could raise wage levels. Servants in receipt of allowances and board wages might have been tempted to cut down on what they ate and drank in order to sell these valuable items to others. However, it is questionable how much food they received and the variations were likely to be substantial from one household to another.

According to one writer, 'It was a common belief among mistresses that however low the standard of food and bodily comforts meted out to a servant in the house of a gentleman, they were bound to be far superior to those received by the servant in her own home'. Allowances were therefore measured by the standards that employers considered to be fit for servants and these would differ greatly from the standards they considered to be suitable for themselves.

Some households were well known for providing poor food to their servants. A page boy working in Glynliven (Glynllifon) Caernarfonshire wrote:

'Strangely the food at Glynliven was not good, consisting for the most part of a plain unappetising succession of stew-like meals. When I was first there we were only served one pudding a week, rice on Sundays, tacky stuff. Whether our old gentleman suddenly thought we'd moved into enlightened times I don't know but after I'd been there a year we were allowed stewed fruit every Wednesday.'[3]

Mr Wynn of Glynllifon seemed to be a rather strange man from the accounts of his second footman, Edwin Lee. He described him in this way:

'Mr Wynn was easy to serve but he had his peculiarities. One that I found irrititating and disturbing was that he always spoke to the servants with his back to them. It was almost as if we were strange creatures that he couldn't bear to look at. It was probably because he felt no kind of affinity with the likes of us and this made him nervous and shy. He would bark when things went wrong but a barking back is not frightening, it needs an angry face to go with it.'

There are some interesting examples of deductions being taken from the wages of servants. For example, the Gwredog records show that sums of between 6d. and 2s. were taken half yearly for the Bible Society or for the missionaries. There is also a note from the employer saying, 'and what I have paid for the Patriotic Fund over the servants.'[4]

Wages were paid out on a half yearly basis following the pattern of the hiring fairs in November and March. Agreements were probably reached early on about what deductions were to be taken from the wages of the servants. One assumes that these were agreed on a voluntary basis but it is possible that some employers did encourage their servants to subscribe to certain religious publications or societies.

The standard of the accommodation offered to servants would vary widely. Country houses were generally designed around the comfort of the owners and the living quarters

---

[3] P Sambrook, *Keeping Their Place, Domestic Service in Country Houses*, (2007), p.110
[4] Bangor University, Gwredog MSS, 37.

of the servants were away from the main building. Housekeepers and cooks were normally given their own bedrooms. In addition, housekeepers were given a sitting room which was also used as an office. The Lady's maid was situated as close as possible to her mistresses and nursemaids close to their charges.

The junior staff often shared the same bed. The question of how these women coped with the lack of privacy is very interesting. Most would have had limited living space with their families and being in close contact with other staff at work may have been comforting. The harsh demands of the job may indeed have been made more tolerable if strong friendships were formed between women servants. But life could be very difficult if conflicts occurred in these closed worlds with their lack of privacy.

In these highly structured work environments one would expect servants to move up the ranks over time. Because the records are not continuous on the Anglesey estates, it is difficult to establish patterns of promotions, wage increases or length of service. Certain observations can be made on the basis of the available material but they are very tentative. Charles Booth, the nineteenth century reformer who documented working class life, found in his survey of domestic servants in London that promotion within the same household was rare; it was more likely that a new servant was brought in rather than an existing one being promoted. Lynne Haims came to a similar conclusion on the basis of the evidence she found. For example, she found that of the 49 housekeepers in her survey, 6 were promotions (1 cook, 1 housemaid, 2 nurses and 2 town housemaids). Of the 102 cooks, 5 were promotions (2 kitchenmaids, 2 upper kitchen maids and 1 housemaid). Haims also found numerous examples of servants who served many years in the same household but who received no salary increases. For example, Mary Hislop served 15 years (1883 -1878) as housekeeper at

Holker at a rate of £55 0s. 0d. per annum. Also, Mary Keating served 11 years (1857-1888) as first laundry maid at Stoneleigh Abbey at a rate of £20 0s. 0d. per annum.[5]

No evidence came to light in Anglesey of promotions being given to the female members of staff. Indeed, in line with the findings of Haims, there are cases of servants being employed in the same capacity, for similar wages over a long period of time. For example, at Plas Newydd a housemaid called Jane Evans first came into the wage records in 1817. At this time she was earning 12 guineas per annum. She was still there in 1832 in the same capacity and earning the same amount of money. She must have been a satisfactory worker because in 1847 it was noted that she was given a pension by her employers. It is difficult to understand why she did not progress up the ranks. [6]

At Baron Hill two housemaids, Jane Jones and Margaret Jones came up continuously in the records for board wages from 1841 to 1849 without any apparent change in their position. [7]

The Henllys papers provide an interesting example of a household that did raise the wages of servants. The records only run for twelve years and are fragmented, but it is striking to note how fussy the employers were in their choice of servants. They were hired on a half yearly term, running from November to May and May to November, and there was a constant turnover of staff. For example, between 1830 and 1835 six housemaids were hired for a term and were dismissed at the end of the six months. Reasons were given in two of the cases; one of the housemaids was dirty and the other was 'a great talker'. In the same period two housemaids were hired for a year and then discharged.

---

[5] L. Haimes, op cit., p.256
[6] Bangor University, Plas Newydd MSS., 2, 3333; 3, 5189; VII, 3111, 3106, 3110.
[7] Bangor University, Baron Hill MSS., 6893

Wage rises and presents were given to the staff who proved to be satisfactory to the employers. For example, the lady's maid who was hired in 1839 at a rate of £10.0s.0d. per annum had her wages increased to £14.0s.0d per annum. This was done as 'some trifling acknowledgement of the attention paid to my dear wife.' It was raised again to £16.0s.0d. per annum with a note that it was 'justly due for the care taken in my absence.' A housemaid who was hired in 1838 at a rate of £8.0s.0d. per annum had her wages raised to £8.10s.0d. in 1839; to £9.0s.0d. in 1840 and to £10 0s.0d. a year in 1841. She was also given a gift of 10s. in 1840 for 'good conduct.' Finally, a kitchen maid who was hired in 1836 at a rate of £5.0s.0d. per annum which was raised to £5.5s.0d. in 1839 and again to £6.0s.0d. in 1840 for 'good conduct.' For the same reason she was given 10s. by her master and 10s. by her mistress in 1840 and by her master again in 1841. Her wages continued to rise until they reached £8.0s.0d. per annum in 1842.[8]

It is clear from the Henllys papers that women were automatically dismissed or chose to leave when they became married.

The Gwredog papers show that servants were hired on a half-yearly basis and even when servants were kept on for longer they were entered in the records as 'hired' from one date to the next. This suggests that the contracts were in effect renewed every six months so that some negotiations may have been entered into on these occasions about wages. This practice could have been difficult for servants if it was used to threaten them with termination of their contracts.

Length of service may be viewed, to some degree, as an indicator of servant attitudes towards their employers although it is impossible to give accurate information from

---

[8]   Bangor University, Henllys MSS., 211

the scant evidence. There were two general trends at work – one showing a stable, long-term employment pattern and the other short-term employment whereby a servant stayed with the same employer for a period ranging between 3 months to 18 months. A survey in 1899 of 1,864 households in London and 2,443 households throughout England and Wales showed that servants spent an average of just over three years in the same household.[9] Lynne Haims in her survey found that the average length of service for all female servants was 2.5 years with over 60% staying in one household less than two years.[10]

There are local examples which suggest that some degree of deviance was tolerated by employers if they wanted to keep staff. For example, the housekeeper who was at Penrhos in 1807 was subject to occasional 'drunken fits' which lasted three or four days. There is no indication that she was punished or that her job was threatened as a result of this behaviour.[11]

Another example from Penrhos later in the century shows that employers were sometimes prepared to go to some lengths to keep their staff. Jane Adeane mentions an occasion in November 1886 when a family member named Rosalind was expected to arrive at Penrhos on that Saturday but a telegram had arrived saying that she would be late. Jane Adeane explained the situation.

The explanation was that when she (Rosalind) reached Carlisle she opened the letters that she had put unopened into her bag and found among them one from the cook giving warning of leaving. So back to Naworth she had to go to get the cook to stay. All ended right, the cook stayed; the report is that her only grievance was that she had not an armchair in the kitchen.[12]

---

[9] T. McBride, op cit., p.58

[10] L.Haimes, op cit., p.259

[11] Bangor University , Penrhos Papers, III, 405

[12] Bangor University General Collection, 32169, p.164

These cases stand out as exceptions to the rule and it is likely that there were particular reasons why they received this special attention. The case of the cook fits other evidence which suggests some mistresses were in awe of their cooks and therefore very keen to keep them.

The Anglesey Agricultural Society gave prizes or premiums (preimin in Welsh) at the annual show for a range of activities including long service by servants. These were given to farm labourers and dairymaids and two servants from Baron Hill were awarded prizes for long service. In 1886, John Jones, servant in husbandry was given three sovereigns for 'having faithfully served there upwards of 19 years'. In 1838, Jane Hughes, dairymaid was given two sovereigns for long service 'upwards of 22 years' at Baron Hill. A note in the accounts books refers to Jane Hughes, dairymaid, in 1846 when she was given a new gown 'for making good calves'. This brought her length of service up to nearly thirty years.

Long service was rewarded in some cases by servants being given a pension in their old age. A study of the Beaumaris Poor Law highlights the difficulties faced by the elderly and infirm and a very high value would be placed on receipt of such payments from employers. In the Baron Hill account books an entry in 1800 stated, 'a quarters pension to the old cook up to 10 February'. There is also a note in the same year which states, '£1 to a late servant in distress at Coventry', showing that this past servant had written to her old employers when in need of help.

The name 'Jane Evans housemaid' appeared on a regular basis in the Plas Newydd accounts in the 1820s and in 1847, listed as 'pensioner'. The following entry stated that, 'December 29 1847 Bill worth £1.10.0 for repairing house of Jane Evans pensioner West Gate House (Window frames repaired) and December 31st 1847 Jane Evans receiving quarterly pension of £5.4.0.' [13]

---

[13] Bangor University, Henllys MSS., 211

Vails or tips were another potential source of extra income for servants working in aristocratic establishments. However female staff did not usually benefit as much as men from this custom. Arthur Munby noted an example in his diary of the way the custom worked and how unfair it was to women servants. He said:

'And in the hall was the nameless buxom kitchen maid, who had exerted herself to get me a hot breakfast and even to bring it in. Yet my vail was given only to Thomas the footman, who did nothing but brush my coat. Such is the force of circumstance.' [14]

Occasional references in the Anglesey estate records suggest that the practice of giving tips or gifts to the servants of friends was common on the island. In the Baron Hill account books there are entries that record that sums of around £1.1s.0d. were paid out to servants in other houses. An entry in the Penrhos estate account books reads, 'August 5th 1840: Paid the servants of Gwredog 3s.6d.' [15]

Some servants were left articles of clothing, allowances or sums of money in the wills of their employers. Mary Jones of Gwredog in 1892 included her servant in her will saying:

'If my servant who has been in my service for upwards of twenty-five years should be alive at my decease I will and direct that the sum of fifty pounds free of duty be paid to her.' [16]

The Meyrick estate of Bodorgan was on a scale similar to Plas Newydd with an acreage in the mid eighteen thirties of 14,000, and in the estate papers the will of Mrs H. Meyrick includes the following statement about her servants.

---

[14] Quoted in L Haims, op cit., p.267
[15] Bangor University, Penrhos Papers, 3 198
[16] Bangor University, Gwredog MSS, 785

'To my maid servant Grace Jones, if she lives with me at the time of my Death, the sum of forty pound and the apparel I have in wear. To my maid servant Jane George if she lives with me at the time of my death the sum of £40 and I desire that each of my servants may have decent mourning.' [17]

References or characters from the landed gentry could be very important for servants who wanted to move on to gain better positions. There was no legal requirement for an employer to give a character reference. Indeed, if the employer wished to be vindictive by refusing to give one, it could deprive the servant of her livelihood. Two local examples from the Penrhos papers and Bodorgan papers reveal the worry it caused servants.

To The Right Honourable Lord Stanley
My Lord,
I beg to apply for my daughter Susan's character, which I understand you kindly promised.
Your Lordship will probably think it strange that I should ask for it now, since she left Penrhos 6 months ago. She got a good place in about a month after coming home, but her friends are anxious that your Lordship should bear testimony of her honesty in performing her duties in Penrhos for 10 years. It will be some consolation to herself as she still feels her sudden dismissal a great trial, and it will satisfy the curiosity of many, as it created no little surprise, so I shall feel most grateful to your Lordship if you will forward the character to my address.
I am your Lordship's humble servant
I. Elwy Jones
Elwyfa St Asaph.
June 18 1898. [18]

---

[17] Bangor University, Bodorgan Papers, 711
[18] Bangor University, Penrhos VIII, 253

In the Bodorgan Papers (uncatalogued), there is a voucher dated August 1830, which reads:

'As Abigail Gibson was not received into Mrs Fullers service without a written character, which she brought with her, as well as Letters previously wrote on the subject, she therefore begs that Mrs Fuller will be so good as give her one stating the fault from which she is turned away'.

The other feature that marked out service in the homes of the wealthy was the prospect of travel for some servants. The lifestyle of the aristocracy centred around the need to socialise in the most fashionable settings and this could involve considerable travel. The local records do contain many references to travelling expenses which took the form, for instance in the Penrhos papers, 'fares of servants railway to London, £12. l5s. 0d. Other entries are far more extensive as the following example from the Bodorgan records show:

Abigal Gibson (Dairymaid) Expenses from Irvine in Scotland to Bodorgan in Anglesey. [19]

November 18th 1829
November 13th
Paid for coach from Irvine to Glasgow

Outside the coach	£0.	6s.	6d.
Paid for dinner		1s.	0d.
Tea and bed		1s.	6d.

November 14th

Breakfast	1s.	0d.
Dinner	1s.	0d.
Carriage of chist (chest)		

---

[19] Bangor University, Bodorgan Papers (uncatalogued)

There are a number of references in the Plas Newydd papers to expenses for servants travelling to and from Beaudesert, Staffordshire, the family's other estate. A reference in the the diary of William Bulkeley Hughes in the Plas Coch collection reveals that servants sometimes travelled abroad. In this case they went to Geneva at a cost of nearly £500. [20]

Lower ranked servants were less likely to travel. For women from small communities, the prospect of travelling to London for example would have been very exciting. There is an unusual example of a kitchen maid, Annie Evans, travelling from Penrhyn Castle to London in 1900.[21] She recalls:

'We used to go to London quite often, to Lord Penrhyn's London house. We travelled second class – there were three classes then. This was particularly when Lord Penrhyn was attending the House of Lords.'

There were clearly huge benefits for the staff who found employment in these stately homes. Social interactions, the possibility of travelling with the family and the likelihood of receiving at least a minimum level of comfort in terms of food and accommodation would have made these roles highly desirable. Social events for staff were organised in some households. At Penrhyn Castle for example in the early 1900s, the butler, Mr Sharpe arranged dances in the steward's room every month with a band from Bangor.[23]

A critical consideration in looking at the advantages for servants of working in the homes of the wealthy is just how many women were afforded this opportunity and how many of them were local to Anglesey? This sheds light too on the larger role of the estates in the local economy. For

---

[20] Bangor University, Plas Coch MSS., 2, 3897
[21] S. Evans, op cit., p. 140
[23] Ibid., p.160

instance, how far did the wealth of the owners find its way into the local community in the form of wages paid out to workers or in money paid to local farmers and traders for provisions? This is not the prime focus here but in looking in such detail at the records of the estates certain observations can be made. As would be expected, the estates relied heavily on the money they gained in the form of rents and the cheap supply of labour. This was particularly evident in a community where few alternatives existed for employment. There is case for suggesting that they received much more from labour and rents than they ever gave back in wages or charity.

The records do not suggest that any great advantages were gained by local traders in having the gentry living on their doorsteps. The major families on the island spent time in residence in other places and occasions when large numbers of people were in residence locally were limited. These would have been the peak periods when local traders were most likely to sell their goods to the gentry and aristocracy. However, the amount of local produce which was purchased was likely to be limited because the home farms would have provided a great deal of the food consumed. The Penrhos papers show that local produce was sent weekly to the family when they were in London or Cheshire. In terms of furniture, furnishings and clothing, fashion would have dictated that such items be bought in exclusive shops in England. The estates were largely self-sufficient units and the wealth which was generated from them did not necessarily find its way into the local economy; on the contrary, a great deal of it went out of the county and, indeed, out of Wales.

Opportunities for local women and girls to enter the 'big house' were also extremely limited from the records seen here. This echoes the findings of other historians. For example, Lynne Haims examined the origins of servants in large country houses to establish whether local people who grew up in their shadow ultimately took up employment there. She found in 1851 that out of 375 female servants in her study, only 30 or 8% came from the parishes within which the country houses were situated. A larger number, 40.8% came from other parishes within county boundaries. In 1861, the figures were 3.9% and 36.8% and in 1871 4.8% and 29.7% In addition, she found that upper servants were less likely to be local born. In 1851, in her survey, only 2.9% upper servants came from the same parish and only 15.7% from anywhere in the same county. In 1881, no upper servants in her sample of 98 came from the same parish and only 16.3% from the same county. In 1871, 1 out of 105 came from the same parish and 9.6% from the same county.

By contrast, 41 out of 553 (7.7%) of lower servants came from the same parish in 1851 and 42.3% from anywhere in the same county. In 1861, the figures were 6.5% and 40.2% and in 1871. 5.2% and 33.2%[24] Overall, the figures show a very low rate of local employment in country houses. The figures are higher within county boundaries but even here, well over 50% of the female staff moved from other areas to take up positions. This evidence tells us something about the attitudes of the wealthy classes towards their local community but it also reinforces a previous point made about migration patterns. Female domestic servants were a highly mobile group of workers and this consideration has been under-played in studies of migration where the emphasis has been placed on male workers moving to industrialised areas.

This local research supports the view that the large estates did not in general employ local women, particularly in the higher ranking roles within the servant hierarchy. In Plas Newydd, which was a substantial estate on the island, most of the indoor staff came from England. The family spent most of their time in their other country home in Staffordshire. A useful document in the Plas Newydd papers

---

[24] L. Haims, op cit., p.60

shows, what looks like, the full complement of staff in 1616 which comprises 17 females and 17 males. All except two have English surnames and Elizabeth Jones, the most likely to have been local from Anglesey, was a low ranking laundry maid. All the servants travelled with the family from Staffordshire to Anglesey and Beaudesert was clearly the base from which staff were recruited. Only a skeleton staff of local servants was kept at Plas Newydd to keep the place in order. Only two housemaids were employed in this capacity, one who lived in and one who came in every day. Opportunities for promotion were very slim for such domestics; they were not seen as part of the main body of staff. Their role in the estate organisation was very different from the core staff that moved around with their employers.

It is difficult to establish from the records whether opportunities did arise for local staff to move with the employers. There is one example in the Penrhos papers of a servant being considered for a place in the family home in Cheshire. The housekeeper wrote to Lady Stanley in 1819 saying:

'In regard to a Scullery Maid, the Girl which was here last year for the Last five or six weeks has applied for the Places she is a very good working girl and Speaks good English. I long wished her to have gone into Cheshire with your Ladyship Last Year which I think since she is sorry she did not except the offer in Respect to wages she wants four Guineas for this half year and if your Ladyship takes her into Cheshire she hopes the next year to have five Guineas I shall not agree with her till I hear from your Ladyship again'. [25]

The reference here to the ability to speak English is significant and may point to another limiting factor for local women in terms of finding employment or in progressing

---

[25] Bangor University, Penrhos Papers, VIII, 165

through the ranks. The Stanleys, it seems were keen on their staff speaking English because there is another example of the issue of language coming up in relation to staff recruitment. In a letter in 1819 Elizabeth Sainsbury the housekeeper wrote to Lady Stanley saying:

'the Boy John Williams we would take into the house if your Ladyship approved of it as I think there would be a boy wanted in the place of Owen when the Family were here. He understands English tolerably and by being in the House he would get instructed in it.' [26]

The shortage of material locally makes it impossible to give anything but an impression on the recruiting preferences of the aristocratic families on the island. The pattern that Lynne Haims discovered in her study of higher ranking staff being less likely to be local than lower ranking staff has some significance for the Anglesey estates. The general impression is that very few local women were employed as indoor servants in the larger estates like Plas Newydd and Baron Hill. Of those who were employed, their prospects of being promoted or of being taken on by the families in their other residences were slender.

The practice of employing servants from outside the locality was not restricted to the major estates. At Plas Coch, an estate comparable with Henllys, one of the housemaids came from Doncaster in 1827.[27] Also, the lady's maid who was appointed the same year at a rate of 20 guineas per annum, was called Elizabeth Eustace which, from the surname, suggests she was likely to have been English. The housekeeper was called Mrs Mathews and she received £25.0s.0d. per annum and 'to be found in tea and sugar'.

Another estate from within Wales, Erddig in Wrexham followed the same pattern of recruiting from the outside.

[26] Bangor University' Penrhos Papers' VIII, 155
[27] Bangor University, Plas Coch MSS., 2824

Very detailed records of servants and their backgrounds have been undertaken in relation to the estate and it is clear that the family preferred to recruit from outside the locality. One of the reasons given is that the family wanted to avoid gossip from the house being carried to the local community. This is likely to have been an important consideration for many of the wealthy families of the time.

As employment opportunities began to expand for women towards the end of the nineteenth century and servants became far less plentiful, the attitudes of the wealthy families appear to change. Based on oral evidence from Erddig and Penrhos in Holyhead, the employers invested more in local families seen to be loyal and trustworthy. Members of the same family would be employed in different roles and their children would then follow them in later years. The 'servant problem' will be discussed more fully later but it is worth noting this response to the labour shortage as it provided a steady and reliable source for the recruitment of servants. It demanded some investment from employers by providing accommodation or enhanced benefits such as pensions for old age but the advantages were substantial if staff showed loyalty and dedication as seems to have been the case from the evidence found in Erddig and Penrhos.

Attempts have been made to compare wage rates in domestic service with wage rates in other industries. This is a difficult task because of the special nature of domestic service and the inclusion of board and lodging and its value in relation to the price of consumer goods. Ebery and Preston found that the earnings of skilled staff such as housekeepers and cooks kept pace with those paid in the cotton industry. [28] Comparisons when it came to the wages of general servants and lower ranking servants were less favourable. In general

---

[28] M Ebery and B. Preston, Domestic Service in Late Victorian and Edwardian England, 1871-1914, Reading Geographical Papers, (1976), pp 92-94

terms, wages in domestic service did not match the rise in average real wages for men and women in England and Wales in the second half of the nineteenth century.

The local evidence has shown that the opportunities for women in Anglesey to gain positions as skilled servants in the homes of the landed gentry and aristocracy were limited. Placed in the context of the general findings of Ebery and Preston, the local evidence suggests that wages of domestic servants in Anglesey, even in the homes of the wealthy, were below average real wages.

Servants would find it very difficult to protect themselves from poverty if they experienced poor health and the prospect of ageing would be an on-going concern. An example from the Lligwy papers highlights this concern for a servant who wrote to her employer asking for help saying,

'Please Your Majesty
I humbly beg to have some advice to cure some disease that is pricking very painful in my arms it is begin since about 14 years and growing worst still very grievous so painful that I cannot serve the world, and got nothing else to live but my labour like another poor maidservant.
Anne Jones, Rhandir, Llangaffo' [29]

Servants would have attempted to save for these times. The Anglesey Savings Bank which was established in 1818 to offer the 'Industrious and Provident Classes, Particularly to Tradesmen, Servants, Labourers and others, a Secure and Productive Investment for Such Sums as they can Conveniently Spare', show that some female servants were able to save money on their wages. The following example shows the amount of money that Mary Wynne, who was a cook at Penrhos, was able to save and the amount of interest she received on this sum.[30]

---

[29] Bangor University, Lligwy MSS., 1108
[30] Llangefni Archives. WQA/S

1842	December	10th	£12.	0s.	0d.
1843	November	18th	£12.	0s.	0d.
Interest		20th		7s.	4d.

			£24.	**7s.**	**4d.**
1844	March 15th		£6	0s.	0d
Interest				18s.	6d.

			£31.	**6s.**	**0d.***
1845	September 6th Drew Out		£10	0s.	0d.
	November20th Interest			15s.	11d.

			£22.	**1s.**	**11d.**
1846	November 20th Interest			12s.	3d.
Carried over to next book			**£22.**	**14s.**	**2d.**

*Based on Retail Price Index conversion £31.6s.0d is approx £2,770 in today's value.

It would seem that Mary Wynnes's situation was deteriorating between 1842 and 1846 as she was able to make annual contributions of £12 in 1842 and 1843 but only half the amount in 1844 to be followed by a withdrawal in 1845. These savings are not substantial especially as Mary Wynne was employed as a cook. They certainly do not form a very secure basis for old age or illness.

An interesting example of a servant saving for her old age is to be found in Erddig. There is a picture of the housekeeper, Mary Webster, taken in 1852 showing her holding the all-important housekeeper's keys. She was recognised for her thriftiness in her role as housekeeper, but she clearly made many sacrifices in order to save for her old age and, as a widow, to secure her daughter's future. When she died in 1875 and the will was read the Yorke family and staff were shocked to hear how much she had saved over the years. Following the family tradition of writing poems about their servants this one about Mary Webster reveals the sum she had saved.

'A peaceful time she here did spend
And here it did peacefully end.
Few days she on her couch was lain
And passed away without much pain.
At Knockin she was lain to rest
'Midst those with whom she once was blest
And some who longest here had been
Went, and were present at the scene.

At the reading of the Will
In Bank, (we do not mean a Hill,)
Were more than thirteen hundred pounds
'Gainst rainy day! tho strange it sounds
This was by weeping kins-folk claimed,
But whether spent on 'rainy day'
Or a 'fine time' we cannot say.'

These examples are both taken from women in higher ranking roles who had advantages over lower ranking servants both in terms of actual wages and in the 'perks' they received that made it more possible for them to save.

It is clear that life for servants in the homes of the aristocracy and wealthy classes was extremely hard and opportunities for local women were extremely limited. This type of occupation was atypical and we will see in the following section that the norm for most women was far removed from this life. Very young women were sent away from home often experiencing loneliness and 'hiraeth'. Towards the end of the nineteenth century other opportunities opened up for women and the extent to which domestic service was disliked became apparent.

Chapter 4

Middle-Class Mistresses and their Servants

The problem of having limited sources becomes more acute as we move away from the homes of the landed gentry and aristocracy. They formed only a minority of the total servant-keeping class but as wealthy owners of estates they were very good at keeping records of expenditure and there is much valuable information to be found here. The middle and working classes did not keep records in this way or write about their lives and concerns. It is impossible to identify a clear dividing line between the two classes as there are so many variables to take into account. The standard definition for the middle class would include professions, proprietors of land and houses, manufacturers employing two or more hands, farmers and retailers. However, Anglesey was largely an agricultural society in the nineteenth century and the term 'farmer' covered a range of different income groups. Here the middle class will include farmers who owned substantial farms but were not big enough to be considered as estates. At the other end of the scale, the distinction between farmers and labourers is problematic because small farmers often work alongside their labourers so that in financial terms there was very little between them.

Where possible, the census returns have been used to supplement account books and letters to aid the process of defining the class position of the farmers in this study. Some account books of the clergy have also been used for wages of servants and there are difficulties with these sources too, as the financial circumstances of this class varied enormously according to denomination and the positions of individuals within the church or chapel hierarchy.

Mrs Beeton gives a table of the recommended number of servants to suit the different income groups. As we have seen earlier in the case of the aristocracy, employers did not always heed the advice given by Mrs Beeton and the information she gave should be viewed with a degree of caution. The table runs as follows:

About £1,000 a year	Cook, housemaid and perhaps a man-servant
From £750 to £500 a year	Cook and housemaid
About £300 a year	General servant
About £200 a year	Young girl for rough work

Although a crude correlation cannot be drawn between the middle class and servant-keeping, it is generally recognised that servants were seen as a status symbol in the nineteenth century. They had to undertake all the hard work behind the scenes and then display themselves in their afternoon uniforms if visitors came to the house or when the employers entertained in the evenings. Life could be very hard indeed for servants in households when employers were concerned to keep up appearances but did not have the funds to pay for enough servants to provide all these services.

The cook and the housemaid were the two most essential servants in the middle class household. However, their duties included those that were carried out by a number of different servants in aristocratic households.

The cook carried out the duties of the housekeeper as well as those of the kitchen maid and scullery-maid. Pamela Horn points out that, as well as doing the work in the kitchen, she would have to perform duties in the house, such as, sweeping and dusting the dining room, cleaning the grate, lighting the fire and sweeping and cleaning the front hall and front door- step.[1] She would have to rise at 6 a.m. in the summer and 6.30 a.m. in winter so that she could light the kitchen fire and get through her work upstairs before getting the kitchen in order and cooking the breakfast.

Housemaids were the third most numerous category of servants in 1871 and one in three of them was under twenty years of age. Pamela Horn identified the duties of the housemaid as sweeping and dusting the drawing-room, the front hall and the other sitting rooms, as well as to tidy the grates and to light the fires. To clean the carpet she would spread some damp tea leaves over it and would then sweep them up with a small hard brush, working on her knees. Lamp glasses and candlesticks also had to be polished. All this was done between 6.00 am and breakfast time. She would have to carry cans of hot water to the bedrooms for the family to wash. After breakfast she would make the servants' beds, sweep, dust and arrange the rooms and clean the front stairs and front hall. Before making the best beds she would remove the velvet chairs or other furniture likely to be damaged by dust and would put on a special apron to protect the bedclothes from her working apron and dress. Mattresses had to be turned, pillows smoothed and no dust had to be left under the beds. Grates would have to be cleaned, fires lit, and slops emptied. All basins, water jugs and chamber pots had to be washed and scalded when necessary. Windows also had to be kept clean. Once a week each bedroom had to be

---

[1] P. Horn, op cit., p.61

cleaned thoroughly including washing the paintwork and shaking the curtains. Beds had to be kept clear of bugs and this was a constant battle for the housemaid. If fires were kept in the bedrooms during the day, it was the housemaid's duty to look after them and this included filling the coal shuttles throughout the house. In the evening she prepared the bedrooms, turned down the beds, filled the jugs with water, closed the curtains and took up a can of hot water for each person to wash along with a warming pan or hot Water bottle. The housemaid also had to make sure that each bedroom was supplied with soap, candles, clean towels, writing paper and anything else required. All the time she was carrying out these duties she had to respond promptly to her employers when they rang for her. [2]

The point was made in the previous chapter that employers were reluctant to invest in labour saving devices and this applied with even greater force in the homes of the middle classes.

Families with children were also likely to employ a nursemaid if they could afford it. This kind of work was often carried out by very young women and over half of all nursemaids in the middle years of the nineteenth century were under the age of twenty. Their duties according to Pamela Horn included dressing and undressing the children, playing with them and taking them out for walks. [3] The amount of time that nursemaids spent with their charges would vary according to the circumstances of their employers and their attitudes towards the care of children. In some cases, nursemaids looked after children for long periods in households where both parents worked, for instance, in small businesses or on farms.

The general servant or maid-of-all-work was also employed in some middle class households. This was the

[2] Ibid., pp. 64-65
[3] Ibid., p.66

lowest ranking occupation in domestic service. Also, the largest numbers of servants were to be found in this occupation. In 1851 there were 575,182 general servants compared to 48,648 housekeepers, 44,009 cooks and 49,885 housemaids. In 1871 there were 780,040 general servants compared to 140,836 housekeepers, 93,067 cooks and 110,505 housemaids. [4]

The lives of general servants or maids-of-all-work were, without a doubt, very hard indeed. They could of course find themselves working with employers who treated them with respect and consideration. However, at the worst end of the scale their lives can be described as nothing less than enslavement in conditions of absolute exploitation.

In addition to the amount of work they had to undertake and the monotony of their daily round of chores, they also had to deal with the isolation of being set apart from their employers without the company of other servants. Charles Booth commented on the lot of the general servant saying, 'The dullness which is the complaint universally urged against single-handed places of all kinds is felt very keenly by children of fifteen or so; they have always been accustomed to living in a crowd, and are frightened by the loneliness of the long evenings in which they sit in the kitchen by themselves, or perhaps to be left entirely alone in the house.' [5]

Their work routine was punishing as is shown in this local example of the duties of a general servant in 1890 in Bryn Bella, Penmaenmawr, part of the estate of Mr Elias Jones of Gwredog.[6]

8 a.m. Get up. Clean all the ashes out of the range.
Clean the tops of the oven. Polish it with a black lead brush.
Polish the steel part with paraffin & soot

---

[4] J.Burnett, op cit., p.138
[5] Quoted in J Burnett, op cit., p.170
[6] Bangor University, Gwredog, uncatalogued

Clean fender, fire irons with the same and put away under the table until the afternoon.

Clean the plate rack and polish the steel front of it.

Make a fire and fill the kettle with fresh water.

Make a fire in the dining room.

Black lead and polish what is necessary.

Dust the dining room.

Dust the table and legs of chairs and floor, the grate, as well as the more important furniture.

Sweep the crumbs around the table with dust pan and brush. (after every meal).

Lay the table

Take her own breakfast.

After taking in breakfast to the dining room, sweep the hall, shake the mats and wash the door steps.

Then clear the breakfast, tidy the dining room.

Wash breakfast things.

Clean saucepans and knives.

Tidy kitchen and scullery.

Prepare dinner.

Clean herself and put on a clean apron.

Take a jug of boiling water and a cloth and duster upstairs.

After emptying the slops, scald the vessels with boiling water and wipe them dry.

Make the beds with a bedroom apron on, made round and wide and with a bib.

Dust the rooms, stairs, closets, hall and furniture.

The mistress to dust the drawing room - the servant to sweep it, clean the windows, grate etc.

Then go down.

Put on a coarse bib apron (turning her white apron to the back) Go to the kitchen and get dinner ready.

After cleaning and washing up fill the kettle with fresh water.

Dress for the afternoon.

In the evening turn down the beds.
Empty slops and draw down the blinds.
WEEKLY WORK
MON Wash and brush out clothes and keep.
TUES Sort out the wash, put aside what wants mending.
Clean our room and dressing rooms.
WED Spare room, servant's room, bathrooms, landing
and stairs.
THURS Drawing room, library.
FRI Dining room,clear shelves.
SAT Kitchen, scullery, hall, and garden seats.

The number of tasks that had to be performed by one
person is astonishing. The details about exactly what
aprons should be worn for particular tasks highlights the
number of occupations that came under the title of 'general
servant'. Each change of apron symbolizes the different
occupations which, in the homes of the landed gentry and
aristocracy, would have been carried out by a number of
servants. The sheer relentlessness and monotony of the
daily and weekly ritual of housework is also shown up very
clearly in this document.

In discussing servants in the homes of the middle
classes a few examples have been chosen to indicate wage
levels in Anglesey to form a basis for comparison with
wages of servants in wealthier households. Caera, a farm in
Llanfair-yng-Nghornwy, according to the census schedules
of 1881, consisted of 300 acres employing 8 men and two
boys. The female staff in 1881 comprised an unmarried
housekeeper from Scotland aged 29; a married dairy maid
from Anglesey aged 23, and an unmarried housemaid from
Llanfair-yng-Nghornwy aged 27. In 1871, the female staff
had all been different comprising a house maid, dairymaid
and kitchen maid who were all unmarried and aged under
25 yrs of age and a governess who was a 'certified teacher
from Liverpool'. In 1881, there was one local, unmarried

housemaid aged 38. The account book for 1878 lists some wages that were paid to servants in that year. For example:

Ellen Dixon at £8. 0s. 0d from May to November. Paid in full and left.
Margaret Davies at £5. 0s. 0d. from May to November. Paid in full and left.
Sophia Williams at £4. 0s. 0d. from May to November. (There are deductions from her wages for 10s. 0d. for shoes; ls. 0d. fair; 2s. 6d. for shoes; 15s. 0d. For stays; and another 5s. 0d. for stays.)
Betsan Jones from November to May at £6. 0s. 0d. (There are deductions from her wages for 2s. 6d. a seat in chapel; ls. 2d. a looking glass; 3s. 6d. an umbrella; 7s. 6d. shoes; sixpence chapel; two entries for 10s. 0d. a time 'on account'. [7]

It would seem that the turnover of servants was frequent in Caera by the references to 'paid in full and left', and the fact that none of the servants mentioned in the 1871 and 1881 censuses was present in 1878. In 1881, the wages paid to servants ranged between £4. 0s. 0d. and £8. 5s. 0d. a half year.

The diary of Thomas Williams a farmer from Llanfairpwll contains the following entry in 1899 which points to the difference between the role of the housekeeper in a smaller establishment and the same position, by name, in the homes of the wealthier classes.

December 1899 The maid Grace of Amlwch (21) — Ellen set her to her duties — as housekeeper £7 — gave her 1/3 to "bind" her from Amlwch — declares she's up to all work. [8]

---

[7] Bangor University, Caera Papers. 9.
[8] Bangor University, General Collection, Vol VIII, 8469-8475

The reference to 'binding' is a form of contract that was entered into where the servant promised to serve for a period, likely to be of six months duration, on receipt of an agreed sum of money from the employer.

The account books of the family of Rev. William Roberts, Calvinistic Methodist Minister of Bethesda chapel in Amlwch provide some other examples of wages paid to servants. According to the 1851 census six people lived in the household, William Roberts, Sarah Roberts, his wife, three children and a female servant aged 20 from Amlwch. [9] The family were involved in running a shop in Llanfaethlu which supplied wheat and corn to local farmers and the family records in the name of the son and granddaughter of Rev. William Roberts indicate that the servants were paid at the following rates:

Wages due from 20th May 1885 Susi Owen	£5.	0s.	0d.
Wages due from November 20th Susi Owen	£5.	5s.	0d.
Wages due from May 1886 Susi Owen	£5.	12s.	6d.
Wages due from November 1886 Susi Owen	£5.	15s.	0d.
Wages due from May 1887 Susi Owen	£6.	2s.	6d.
Wages due November 1887 Ellen Thomas	£6.	5s.	0d.
Wages due May 1888 Ellen Thomas	£6.	5s.	0d.
Wages due November 20th 1888 Alice Griffiths			

Alice Griffiths was still employed with the family in 1891 when she received £7. 10s. 0d.

The financial circumstances of chapel ministers sometimes made it very difficult for them to perform their duties in the community. The Rev. William Morgan (1801-1872), a Baptist minister in Holyhead, makes a number of references in his diary to the sad state of his finances. He did not receive enough money to employ a servant. [10]

[9] Bangor University, General Collection, Vol 2, 1104-1108
[10] Bangor University, General Collection, Vol X, 15562
[11] Bangor University, Ashby (Ty Calch) MSS, 60

The letters of Mrs Williams, Ty Calch Bodorgan, who was married to the Rev. W. Williams, reveal the financial difficulties that the family experienced. [11] In correspondence with her son she wrote:

'I do so want to see Taida but am so tied down to this place with only this silly servant girl that really I don't know how to leave.'

On another occasion she wrote:

'the servant woman is gone to her home for a fortnight so that both your Aunt and myself are Drudges doing all manner of dirty work.'

Although she was clearly dissatisfied with the servant, there is no reference to her trying to get someone else to replace her. Also, when the servant went home, no attempt was made to get another servant to stand in while she was away. The tone of the letters suggests that Mrs Williams had known better times and that she was having to adapt to living in reduced circumstances. The letters contain other references to servants which cast an interesting light on the affairs of the chapel 'Society' and the moral conduct of its members. In addition, the occasional references to members of the society who have left for work throw some light on the mobility of servants.

1860
David the Tailor son of Lydia Jones is to be married to Mary the servant of Tan Rallt — the one that we always see on Sundays going to Capel Mawr she is in the family way and both have been turned out of the Society.
1860
the "Revival" is kindling again at Capel Mawr — three joined the Society there this week two of the servants of Fferm ? and Elin, the old servant of Dyffryn.

1860

there is an addition to the Society among others Betsy James who you know is in service in Dublin has returned to the Society after being for two years yn wrthgiliedig (lapsed).

1862

William Bron Haulog has been expelled from the society as the servant of ? is in the family way of him.

1863

Emma Jones is gone to Liverpool in search of a situation as Housemaid.

1863

do not know how to let John (her other son) know my opinion on his living with a servant woman alone in the House.

Mrs Williams herself was struggling emotionally and one letter in particular shows the depth of her depression. She writes:

'I cannot tell you how useless I see myself now – when nursing my children I valued my life as essential to your comfort but now I am only like some others of the Mamalian tribe that are only useful while they suckle their young. I have no mental usefulness to be of any service to any of you now. What am I left for alive.'

These references in Mrs Williams's letters suggest that religious activity was an important element in the lives of some Anglesey servants. It was observed earlier that deductions were sometimes taken from their wages for 'chapel'. The letters also reveal that a strong moral code existed in relation to the sexual behaviour of Society members and that a close eye was kept on the private affairs of members.

The Llaneilian Rectory Accounts are amongst the Caera Papers and they also provide information about the sums paid to servants. For example, in the eighteen-forties they were paid between a £1. 0s. 0d. and £1. 5s. 0d. a half year. [12] By 1867, this figure had risen to £3. 12s. 0d. In 1883, they were paid £5. 0s. 0d. and in 1886, £7. 0s. 0d. It is interesting that wages increased more rapidly towards the end of the century suggesting that servants were in a stronger position to expect higher wages as alternative employment opportunities opened up for women at this time.

There are references again to what was seen as acceptable sexual behaviour. A letter written to the rector of Llaneilian contained the following accusation:

'Dear Sir,
As the rumour, to which I have alluded, was in general circulation, and, I have reason to believe, not unknown to your own friends, I did not think it necessary to enter with the particulars of the charge. But, as you ask for the explanation, I now inform you that the report which has reached me is, that you are the Father of one or more natural children by a maid servant. From the wide currency of this report and the credit which has been paid to it, I cannot but think that some circumstances must have occurred, which have given occasion to the suspicion.'

It seems the Rector of Llaneilian had, rather blatantly, disregarded local opinion.

The wages of servants in these examples can be seen to be generally lower than those paid to lower ranking servants in the homes of the landed gentry and aristocracy. The housekeeper who had been appointed by Thomas Williams, a farmer in Llanfairpwll, in 1899 was paid £7. 0s. 0d. [13] This was the same as the rate paid rate to housemaids in Penrhos at the earlier date of 1854. The wages of

---

[12] Bangor University, Caera Papers, 29
[13] Ibid

servants at Caera were very similar to those paid to servants at Gwredog. A clear line can be drawn between Caera and Gwredog, substantial farms on the island, and the larger estates of Baron Hill, Plas Newydd and Penrhos. The rates of pay of servants in Baron Hill in 1886 stand out as being very much higher than all the other local examples. The fact that servants were recruited from England in this establishment was likely to influence wage rates.

It is interesting to note the relationship between wages and servants being convicted for theft. In a study, by Susan C. Ellis she found that fewer cases of theft can be found amongst servants from higher ranking households. [14] Wages for some servants could be appallingly low. In a local case, a girl at Amlwch Port who was convicted of stealing 6 shillings from her employer, a flour dealer, was paid 6d. a week for her labour. She also points out that servants employed in upper class households were accused of theft less commonly than servants in middle class households. She suggests that this may have been the result of servants being 'paid higher wages in the wealthier households.

From the Anglesey figures, the lowest wages were paid in Llaneilian Rectory in the earlier years but they improved towards the end of the century. The increase in wage levels at this time is consistent with the findings of other historians and was a response to increasing competition from alternative employments such as shop work. The local evidence also supports the findings in other studies suggesting that servants were paid less in middle class households than servants in the homes of the aristocracy.

As noted earlier, the ideas associated with domestic ideology were expressed most clearly in the behaviour and lifestyles of the middle-class. Middle-class women were financially dependent on their husbands and were

---

[14] S.C. Ellis, 'Observations on Anglesey Life 1860-1869', *Transactions of the Anglesey Antiquarian Society*, 1986, pp135-136

supposed to be content to stay at home organising household affairs. Here, she was protected from the corruption and dangers connected with the public world of work. At the end of the working day, the husband would expect to come home to a supportive and attentive partner in a calm and well organised environment.

In order to perform these duties placed upon her, the middle-class mistress required suitable and capable servants. In her role as mistress, she conveyed middle-class ideals to the young women in her employ. Domestic ideology brought with it a new relationship between these women. Some mistresses themselves would be new to their roles. Unlike the aristocracy, they had not been born into wealth and therefore had to learn how to become the perfect wife, mother, home-keeper and keeper of servants. Both mistress and servant were constrained by their financial dependence on the male breadwinner but the servant was doubly constrained because her class position placed her in a subservient relationship to her mistress too.

The abundance of manuals giving advice on household management were a direct response to the needs of these new middle class mistresses. They sought to professionalise and give meaning to the separate sphere of the home. Here women had all the influence and control and were judged on their success or failure by their peers. The professional-isation of house-keeping that was promoted in manuals and magazines mirrored the rationalisation of work practices that was taking place in the factories at the time. Wives were encouraged to adopt, in the home, those methods of management which their husbands were applying in the public arena of work.

Many mistresses, at the beginning of the century, were ill-equipped to deal with these new demands. In the pages of domestic manuals, this was a source of comment throughout the century. The standards set by society for middle-class women were extremely high and the burden must have been heavy for some to meet the expectations that were so firmly placed on their shoulders. Tensions were bound to spill over and influence the relationship between mistresses and their servants. Tensions arising from these pressures on middle class women could then colour the relationships between mistresses and servants.

There is an amusing example of advice being given to middle class women about the virtues of good housekeeping in a moral tale called 'Lily Gordon; or The Young Housekeeper', written by Catherine D. Bell. [15] It is a story about a young girl called Lily whose mother died while giving birth to her. Her father and the rest of her relations spoilt her dreadfully. She was educated by her brother's tutor and Lily, according to the story teller, 'made considerable progress in what I might call the more masculine parts of her education, but of feminine acquirements she really had none'. An aunt of Lily's was very concerned about her education and persuaded her father to send her to school. However, even at the school she was not taught any housekeeping skills . Fortunately, the owner had herself become conscious of the need for such training because she had received a most distressing letter from one her former pupils as a result of her ignorance of household management. The letter contained a catalogue of disasters which occurred when the writer moved to her husband's home on their marriage. For instance, when making a cup of tea for her new husband she poured cold, rather than boiling water, onto the tea leaves. She was quite incapable of controlling the cook who, in the company of guests on a special occasion; served up 'fried fish quite soft and swimming in grease; mutton chops dried and burnt on the outside, raw within; and potatoes in a sort of wet, stickly mass, most uninviting to the eye.'

---

[15] Catherine D. Bell, *Lily Gordon:or The Young Housekeeper*, (no date), inscription dated June 1872

The writer was also lavish in buying provisions when they were out of season and therefore at their most expensive. The outcome of the affair is that the owner of Lily's school decides to give her female students some instruction in the theory of housekeeping and the rest of the book deals with Lily's own experiences of gaining knowledge of household management, and, in particular, learning to deal with servants.

Mrs Beeton also gave advice to mistresses. She wrote:

'The responsibilities or duties of the mistress are, though onerous and important, by no means difficult if given careful and systematic attention. She ought always to remember that she rules the household; and by her conduct its whole internal policy is regulated. She is, therefore, a person of far-reaching importance. Her daughters model themselves on her pattern, and are directed by her counsels. "Her children rise up and call her blessed; her husband also, and he praiseth her". Therefore, let each wife, remembering her responsibilities, see that her conduct is such as to earn the love and reverence of her children and her husband.'

On the section on servants, she says:

'The treatment of servants is of the greatest importance to both mistress and domestics. If the latter perceive that their mistress's conduct is regulated by high and correct principles, they will not fail to respect her; and if a real desire is shown to promote their comfort, while at the same time a steady performance of their duty is exacted, then well-principles servants will be anxious to earn approval, and their respect will not be unmingled with affection.'

It was noted earlier that some publications in Wales were directed at women. *Y Gymraes* and *Y Frythones* certainly promoted domestic ideology but they were periodicals rather than household manuals. Y Gymraes' (The Welshwoman), edited by Ieuan Gwynedd was intended to fill a perceived gap in Wales is such literature. It was noted in the first edition that English women had access to publications like Family Friend, Mother's Magazine, the Family Economist and the Ladies Newspaper. 'Y Gymraes' was published in response to the Education Report of 1847 referred to as the Blue Books (Brad y Llyfrau Gleision / the Treachery of the Blue Books) and the damning criticisms it had made of the immorality of the Welsh. It set out to improve education for women to make them better wives and mothers. Each publication carried articles on good housekeeping and women were given cookery tips.

They ran articles about successful women, mainly in the field of philanthropy. The other group of women who increasingly gained attention were the missionaries who travelled afar to spread the Christian word within the British Empire. These women were clearly stepping out of the restrictions of the hearth and home. But they were exceptional and the role of the Welsh wife and mother continued to be idealised. Sian Rhiannon Williams has made the point that problems such as illness, childbirth and contraception, so central in the lives of working class women, were absent from the pages of these periodicals. [16]

The images of women in 'Y Gymraes', are generally unsympathetic. Sian Rhiannon Williams points in particular to the way farm servants were presented, saying, 'Farm servants, for example, were often portrayed as flighty, irresponsible young girls who spent much of their time courting and committing 'sinful' acts at fairs and in haylofts'. [17]

---

[16] S.R. Williams, Women's Nineteenth-Century Welsh Periodicals, *Our Mother's Land, Chapters in Welsh Women's History 1830-1939*, Ed Angela .V John, (1991), (New edition 2011)
[17] Ibid., p. 76

The 1896 edition of 'Y Gymraes' ran an article on the 'New Woman' (Y Ddynes Newydd). It provides an interesting assessment of the developments that had taken place for women and the emergence of influential women such as Cranogwen (Sarah Rees). She was an exceptional woman who entered a number of areas of Welsh previously closed to women. She was a recognised poet, gave lectures and sermons and was a staunch supporter of the Temperance Movement. She went on to become editor of the Frythones. Much of her teaching was aimed at encouraging working class women to become good wives and mothers, to be content with their position in society and be obedient to their husbands. The author of the article makes it very clear that despite their public spiritedness, women such as Cranogwen were no less 'feminine'. She writes, 'Are women such as Miss Willard and Cranogwen any less useful, any less splendid, any less feminine than those women whose families are the only ones to benefit from their services'.

A prize of twenty pounds was offered at the National Eisteddfod in 1887 for the best handbook on the topic, 'Cookery and Household Management Suitable for the Needs of the the Workers of Wales'. (Goginiaeth a Threfniadaeth Deuluaidd, Cyfaddas i Anghenion Gweithwyr Cymru.) [18] The essay which won first prize was written by a Mrs Edwards who had used the pseudonym, 'Wife of a Welsh Worker'. In the introduction to the book, a brief account is given of why Mrs Edwards' book was chosen. It was praised for its down to earth appeal to people on low incomes.

The existing literature is criticised for being extravagant and working on the assumption that 'the land is flowing with milk and honey' for the poor as well as for the

---

[18] Mrs S.A. Edwards, 'Coginiaeth a Threfniadeth Deuluaidd', Cymdeithas yr Eisteddfod Genedlaethol, (1889)

wealthy. The handbook itself is concerned with bringing order into the routine of housewives. A list is given of essential furniture for each of the rooms in the house and all the items are priced. The list includes what books should be present on the book shelves of Welsh workers; these include mainly religious texts. The emphasis throughout the book is on economy and the need to be methodical. The fact that the project was encouraged in the first place suggests it was a response to a perceived need to improve the general standards of housewifery in Welsh households at this time. Nowhere in the book is there a mention of servants.

It is likely that Mrs Edwards was influenced by her religious beliefs. There is a slightly different slant on domestic ideology here as moral value is given to the wife managing household affairs without the help of servants. The model promoted for the ideal woman discussed earlier is based on her management of the household and servants. Indeed, the less she has to do herself, the more she gains approval and status. This lifestyle was clearly out of reach for many women and the principles being promoted in the essay by Mrs Edwards was probably a lot closer to the reality of life for most. This is particularly likely in rural Wales where the influence of non-conformity was strong and the hiring of servants would be seen as unnecessary, costly and decadent.

Some caution needs to be exercised in looking at the literature that was aimed at women and the attempt to create the 'ideal woman'. Ideas do not remain static and personal circumstances would influence greatly the degree to which women took heed of the advice given to them. Some women may indeed have been resistant to the ideas being put forward and the constraints placed upon them. There are examples too of women who found other outlets to express themselves through philanthropic work.

Chapter 5

The World of Work for the Majority of Girls and Women

It becomes extremely difficult to find information about wage rates, conditions and duties of servants as we move further down the social scale. The majority of girls and women would have found themselves working in single-servant households or alongside family members in low income households. These are the 'silent' majority that are largely hidden from historical records. Sources such as Mrs Beeton's become worthless as a source for this kind of domestic service. In rural locations like Anglesey, many women worked as servants on farms, often combining work in the house with work in the dairy. It is clearly impossible to draw a distinct line between social classes and in some of the discussion that follows, the position of servants will mirror conditions found in lower middle-class households.

For source material it is necessary to look at the agencies that came into contact with servants because they faced such insecurities in their lives. It is to the records of the local workhouses, refuges and charities for the poor that we have to turn to find fragments of information about the hardships faced by this class of servant.

Families with incomes below a hundred pounds a year

would look to institutions for the poor for labour from girls who were desperate for work. Louisa Twining carried out a survey in the 1860s of former workhouse girls to find out what wages they were paid. She found that they received commonly about a pound a year and that very often they did not even receive this meagre amount and many worked for nothing. [1]

Amy Hurlston, a trade unionist testified before a Royal Commission in 1894 that in the Midlands, servants were generally paid two or three shillings a week which was not enough to enable them to join a friendly society. Wages such as this, she said, were commonly paid by small tradespeople.

Servants were also being criticised for their lack of morals and discipline, and their unreliability. Middle class mistresses at the same time were being encouraged to improve standards of housekeeping and charitable work was seen as being compatible with these pursuits. Charitable organisations set out to aid and reform working class girls.

Philanthropic work, often the only occupation open to women of the middle classes, became an important outlet for social interaction and enabled women to feel they were contributing something to the betterment of society. They energetically rose to the task of improving the lot of young servants, teaching them discipline and making them more reliable workers. The number of charitable institutions such as children's homes, refuges and prisoners' aid societies increased dramatically during the second half of the nineteenth century. It has been estimated that by the end of the century out of 1,000 charities, 800 dealt exclusively with girls. Amongst these charities were large institutions that helped domestic servants, for example, the Children's Aid Society, the Ragged School Union, the

---

[1] F.K. Prochaska, 'Female Philanthropy and Domestic Service in Victorian England', *Bulletin of the Institute of Historical Research*, 54, (1981), p. 82

Waifs and Strays Society and the Metropolitan Association for Befriending Young Servants.[2]

Charitable organisations often dealt with the interface between domestic service and prostitution. Prostitutes who were taken into refuges were encouraged to enter domestic service as a more 'acceptable' occupation. Prochaska, has drawn attention to the need to reconsider the relationship between female domestic service and prostitution. The accepted view that the domestic servant class was the greatest supplier of prostitutes, she says, is not supported by the evidence. She suggests that the relationship was the other way round and that prostitutes who were taken into refuges or Magdalene Homes were re-introduced into society via domestic service.[3]

Middle-class women philanthropists, by their efforts, directly influenced the labour market for domestic servants. They succeeded in producing an army of inexpensive servants who were available to a wider range of households. This did not however diminish the outcry from the servant-keeping classes about the unreliability of servants.

A local example of a female philanthropist, may be seen in the case of Jane Adeane of Llanfawr, Holyhead. On the death of her aunt, Ellin Stanley of Penrhos, Jane Adeane adopted a philanthropic role in the locality. Violet Martineau in her portrait of Jane Adeane writes:

'As Penrhos was no longer a permanent home for the owners of the estate, she stepped into the place of Lady Bountiful, and visited the Almshouses, schools, and workhouse, and was always ready to help any philanthropic work, if it was put forward by persons whom she regarded as sound. She had nothing to do with municipal work; she mistrusted Public bodies and never worked them.'[4]

---

[2] Ibid., p.79
[3] Ibid., p.85
[4] Bangor University, General Collection, 32169

This quote points up the limitations of philanthropic work as the choice as to which causes to support was placed entirely in the hands of the individual. Other causes, however important for the members of the community, were therefore neglected if they they did not suit the particular preferences of the individual philanthropist. Municipal work, which Jane Adeane mistrusted, was in principle based on a more democratic structure.

Ellin Stanley had established an Industrial School in Holyhead which had closed shortly after her death. Jane Adeane set about the task of reviving the school and for the purpose, bought a piece of land from the Stanley estate known as Tan Altran in Salt Island where she trained twenty or so girls in domestic work. [5]

Tan Altran was furnished and let to friends and lodgers, who were attended to by the girls as part of their training. They also did all the washing for the Stanley Sailors' Hospital. The girls were orphans or 'Poor Law Girls', who, having completed their training went on to become domestic servants. Unfortunately, no documents were found to shed more light on life in Tan Altran. It remained in existence until the early nineteen twenties and Violet Martineau described the difficulties which Jane Adeane faced in maintaining the home when she wrote:

'The difficulties and expenses had become too great for her to cope with, at 84, and the conditions were far from ideal in 1926, perfect though they seemed in the 'eighties. Tan Altran had done good work and fulfilled a real need'. [6]

Domestic service declined in importance in the period after the First World War and young girls were perhaps less inclined to enter Tan Altran and fit into a structure which was likely to have been very strict and prohibitive.

---

[5] Ibid.
[6] Ibid.

There is other evidence that local pauper children were encouraged to enter domestic service. Flynn-Hughes makes the point that, 'most workhouse children went into service as soon as they were old enough'. [7] In the Bangor Union, the following articles of clothing were given to each child going to service out of the workhouse:

Girls: One bonnet, two aprons, two frocks, two shirts, two flannel petticoats, two upper petticoats, two pairs of stockings, one pair stays, two pairs of shoes.

Boys: One hat or cap, two jackets and two waistcoats, two shirts, two pairs of trousers, two pairs stockings, two pairs shoes.

There are two other local sources that provide some insights into the lives of servants in working class households. The first, the Bastardy Minute Book in the Anglesey Petty Sessions Records, deals with cases where women went to court to get maintenance money from the fathers of their illegitimate children.

Prior to the 1834 Poor Law Amendment Act, mothers of illegitimate children were given out-door relief by the parish and the amount paid out to them was supposed to be given back to the parish by putative fathers. The 1834 Act completely changed this practice so that putative fathers no longer had any legal obligation to repay the parish. The policy makers stated that, 'a bastard will be whatever Providence appears to have ordained that it should be, a burden on its mother and where she cannot maintain it, on her parents'.

The Poor Law Amendment Act of 1844 allowed women the right to appeal to the Justices to make orders against putative fathers if their applications were supported by

---

[7] C. Flynn-Hughes, 'Development of the Poor Laws in Anglesey and Caernarfonshire Between 1815 and 1914'. (MA Thesis, University of Wales, 1945).

corroborative evidence. The Bastardy Minute Book contains records which run from 1856 to 1875 which are mainly concerned with establishing that the defendant in each case is actually the father of the child in question. [8] The women who were asking for orders to be made in their favour had to give details about when and where the couple in question had had sexual intercourse. Witnesses for both parties were then called to verify or deny the charges being made against the accused male. These are substantial books with a large number of cases documented over this period.

The majority of the cases that came up in the Petty Sessions involved domestic servants. Some interesting details emerge about the accommodation which was afforded servants in some of their places of work. It seems that it was common practice to house female servants in the loft or cellar and two or three would often share the same bed. The lack of privacy in these situations meant that couples had 'connexions' in the presence of the servant or servants who were sharing the same bed. This information came out in a number of cases because the servants who had been present during the affairs could then be used as witnesses on behalf of the complainants.

The following example illustrates the point:

Jane Hughes and Owen Jones
Jane Hughes - I was delivered of twin Bastard Children on the 16 August last and Owen Jones now present is the father. He used to visit me at Hendrefn Llansadwrn, we were fellow servants there.

Ann Williams - fellow servant. I am a fellow servant at Hendrefn. I have seen these partners in bed together many times. I was also in bed many times. (Another servant left at the same time as the complainant. They were both pregnant and dismissed.)

---

[8]   Llangefni Archives, Bastardy Minute Books 1856-1875, WU1/63,64,65.

The evidence in these cases has to be viewed with some caution because servants having worked together were likely to support each other. But given the large number of cases viewed, it did seem commonplace for sexual relations between servants to take place in circumstances similar to those described above.

Arrangements were also made between servants to meet, for example, in the kitchen or stable, when the rest of the household was asleep. These arrangements sometimes became long-standing which suggests that servants were very discreet. It is possible too that employers were aware that these meetings were taking place but they chose to turn a blind eye to them.

The records support earlier assumptions that female servants were sometimes expected to enter into sexual relationships with their employers as a matter of course. The most vulnerable servants were those who acted as housekeepers to widowers who became, in effect, substitutes for deceased wives. The impression one gains is that these were very young women who found it difficult to resist the expectations that were made of them.

The following example illustrates the point:

'Ellin Williams and Hugh Salmon (Labourer)
Ellin Williams - servant of the defendant, a widower with 3 children - they are young - the eldest only 10. I was a servant to the defendant and all the domestic work to do. There was a loft in the house, I slept in the scamber (chamber) below stairs, he slept in the loft with the eldest child and the two youngest ones with me - he commenced coming to bed a fortnight after I went there - he used to work away all the week and returned on Saturday spending Sunday at home and he generally slept with me on these occasions - the oldest child that slept with me was a boy aged 9 years. The defendant has promised to marry me but for his first wife's relations - nobody during this time visited me except the defendant. I was there from March 1856 to January 1857, when he turned me away.'

A great deal of information about the conditions of work of servants in working class households can be drawn from this case. As housekeeper, Ellin Williams was entirely responsible for the household including caring for three children. As her employer was away during the week it was unlikely that Ellin had any free time to herself away from her place of work. It is interesting to note that a promise of marriage was made to her as if to legitimise the sexual relationship, but this came to nothing when she became pregnant.

One case in the Bastardy Minutes reveals a situation where the sexual advances of the employer were considered unwelcome by a servant. The employer in this instance was the brother-in-law of the complainant. Female family members were often employed as servants to make up the numbers of females in a household or to replace a central female figure.

The case was described in court in this manner:

'Margaret Williams and William Williams
Margaret Williams - I was delivered of a bastard Child in the 23rd April last and William Williams Tyn-y-Coed Bethedsa Llanllechid Farmer is the father of the Child. I was in service with the defendent in Tyn-y-Coed I was looking after the defendent's children and was housekeeper. He is a widower having married my sister deceased. I started in February 1856 until 23rd July - I became pregnant on that day - at all events it was this day I left - before that he never had connexion with me before but behaved to me like a master - he had only connexion once in his bed. There was only his children in the House that night - the eldest boy about 15 years old. I did not permit him to have connexion willingly - I struggled against him. It was about 4 a.m. It was against my will - I was bruised and cried.

Complainant had come to house of Susan Jones at 8

o'clock in the morning crying saying that William Williams her master was very cruel to her. I took her home. She did not say that he had committed a rape on her.

Her father Hugh Thomas of Pentraeth was present at a meeting between complainant and defendent in his house when defendent had told complainant to come to get her wages - he asked my daughter to come back to finish her half year. She replied that " she would not unless he behaved like a man". He promised solemnly that he would. My daughter came back afterwards. I asked the defendent in my daughter's presence if he would put a lock on my daughter's bedroom door, and he promised to do so and those were the terms on which she was allowed to go back.

The order was refused.'

In another entry from Llandegfan it seems a servant was put under pressure to have sex with her employer. The handwriting in the record is difficult to decipher in places but Elen Oldfield of Tyddyn Bach Llandegfan made a claim in April 1866 against her employer, Thomas Jones of the National School House, Llandegfan. He was the school master. Elen claimed that 'it occurred in his own house' and that 'he had locked the door'. She says that 'I did not struggle but I did not go down willingly'. The case was dismissed for want of corroborative evidence.

There is little doubt that young servants were susceptible to sexual advances by the master of the house and male relatives of the master and his guests. The Minutes of Evidence of the Report for the Select Committee of the House of Lords Relating to the Protection of the Young Girl in 1881 shows that the police were aware of this problem but they found it difficult to convict the master of rape or seduction since, 'the influences possessed by a master over a-young girl prevents that vigorous resistance which would be offered to a stranger'.

The Bastardy Minute Books give a rare insight into many aspects of life for servants and confirm the general theme in this book that large numbers of women were limited to domestic service as the only choice of employment. The references to other occupations are extremely rare. The majority of the cases involved relationships between female servants and other male servants in the same household or nearby, labourers and occasionally quarry workers and stonemasons. A common theme is that women were very often lone servants and this made it very difficult for them to find corroborative evidence and it was left then as the servant's word against the accused male.

Some of these cases are truly tragic showing how few options women had in these difficult circumstances. Many stated that they had moved back to live with their parents on becoming pregnant but clearly this was not always possible and would, in any case, have led to additional pressure being placed on families that were probably already struggling with poverty and overcrowding.

The second source of information is based on the recollections of a domestic servant who worked on a number of farms in Anglesey in the period prior to the First World War. It is drawn from tapes and the written recollections of Mary Elin Jones who was born in Bethel, Trefdraeth in 1886. [9] These recollections are particularly significant because they show us the period prior to the First World War, before the decline of domestic service began. Before this rupture, there was likely to have been a great deal of continuity in the nature of domestic service in the nineteenth century and the early part of the twentieth century in a rural location like Anglesey. The material is in Welsh and, where appropriate, original phrases have been included in brackets.

---

[9] I am extremely grateful to the late Tomos Roberts (Archivist and Bangor University Archives) for granting me access to this valuable source based on recordings of his grandmother Mary Elin Jones.

Mary Elin was twelve years old when she first went into service at a nearby farm in Trefdraeth. There were four other servants at the farm, the head maid (morwyn briws, morwyn llanciau neu y forwyn fawr) and three male labourers. Mary Elin was hired to look after the six children in the household. The head maid was a very dominant figure who was very cruel to Mary Elin both emotionally and physically. She told lies about her to the mistress saying that she was a liar and a thief. The situation eventually forced Mary Elin to leave although it is clear from the records that breaking a contract (torri tymor) mid-term was not taken lightly by her. The employers took the side of the head maid against Mary Elin but they were later proved wrong when they realised for themselves that the head maid was at fault and she was later dismissed.

Mary Elin then moved on to a position on a farm called Treruffydd in Tŷ Croes. She worked for an old lady of eighty-two who was like a mother to her and who taught her a great deal about domestic work. She was occasionally given a white threepenny piece which she divided up. She gave a penny to chapel, another penny to Sunday school which left her a penny to spend on sweets. This underlines how very young she was and that having sweets was such a treat for her. She was paid thirty shillings a half year but most of this went to her family.

Mary Elin was described as a 'kitchen maid' and she worked under the head maid whose responsibility it was to cook for the male labourers. (morwyn llanciau) She was unlucky here too because the maid was again cruel and used to beat her. She had a number of boyfriends and wanted Mary Elin to join her to make foursomes. When she refused the maid became angry and vindictive.

On one occasion, the head maid was caught asleep on the sofa with one of her boyfriends and when the master discovered them, he threw cold water over them and gave the maid the sack.

The duties of the kitchen maid were more wide-ranging than just working in the kitchen. They included cleaning the house, looking after the calves and assisting with the milking and butter-making. The house was very old fashioned and the old lady had a spinning wheel which she worked by candlelight making sheets which were of a rough texture like towels.

When she was about fourteen Mary Elin went to work for one of the daughters of Treruffydd who had a four month old son. Her time was not happy in this position because her mistress was very distressed and emotionally unstable. Viewing the situation from a modern perspective, it looks very likely that her mistress was suffering from post-natal depression. The mistress tried to strangle Mary Elin in the night and was later taken to a mental hospital.

The next position which Mary Elin took up was in a guest house in Rhosneigr. The work was very hard and she was up at six and did not finish until ten at night.

The details of her next position on a farm called Gwna Fawr are incomplete. She stayed there for two years which appears to have been longer than her stay in other places. The pattern had been established whereby she stayed in a place for a contract period of six months and then moved on to a new position.

After Gwna Fawr she went to work in Glantraeth which was about ten minutes away from her home. She was seventeen by this time and was working for a large family where there was always plenty of work to do. Her work was spread over the house, the kitchen and the dairy. She noted that here was always a great deal of washing to be done as well as breadmaking. She used to bake three times a week and made twenty-three loaves at a time. Flour cost a shilling for 7lbs. The bread was kneaded last thing at night and left until the morning when the oven was lit and the task of baking would begin. Eight loaves of bread were baked at a time. When the bread was first put in the oven, the mistress would look after it while Mary Elin and the other maid went to do the milking. When they returned, they ate their own breakfast and then carried on with rest of the morning's work.

Churning was done every day and Mary Elin helped by cleaning out the utensils that were being used. Butter-making was very skilled work and Mary Elin did this work on her own for the first time in Glantraeth. Overall, Glantraeth had been a good place and she had enjoyed her time there and had acquired a number of important skills. It is interesting to follow her progress because she was taking on more responsible positions as she moved around from one place to another. She maintained contact with the families in the places where she had been happy. The movement from one farm to another was within a small radius of her home and it was a very close community at that time. Local people were dependent for work on a small number of farmers. For example, Mary Elin's mother had been going to Glantraeth for a long time to do the washing and Mary Elin herself went back there on a casual basis after she had married.

Mary Elin went back to Treruffydd to work when she was twenty-one. This time she was employed as 'head maid'. The old lady had died and her son owned the farm. He was unmarried (hen lanc) and had employed a housekeeper to run the house, look after the dairy and supervise the female staff. Mary Elin had a great of respect for her and admired the way she tackled all the work she had to do each day. She was the master's niece which again illustrates how common it was for female relatives to take up positions with family members, often fulfilling the role of the deceased wife. She was referred to by Mary Elin as an 'old maid', and it seems that she remained at Treruffydd for many years. This illustrates that servants did show great loyalty to their employers when they were treated with respect.

The housekeeper was responsible for butter-making and Mary Elin describes the process saying that the churn was in use every day. The churn held sixteen gallons of liquid and it was extremely difficult to clean because it was fixed to the floor. There are many interesting details too about the diet of servants and methods of cooking. Most of the cooking was done in a large pot (crochan) over the fire. This pot was in constant use and meals had to be planned carefully because of having only one pot to cook with.

The day started with providing breakfast for the staff and this had to be on the table by 5.30 in the morning. It was common in Anglesey for farmers to put their clocks forward half an hour, so that according to the clock it was six o'clock. The staff consisted of the head of the male staff (hwsmon), two carters, (certwyr), second labourer (ail was), feeder (porthwr), two rabbit catchers and the stable boy. For breakfast they had bread and butter milk (bara-llaeth), which had been soaking overnight. The head of the male staff cut the bread and the butter (brechdanau o fenyn) which was placed on a trencher so that everybody could help themselves. A cup of tea was on offer and the butter which the men ate was generally not fresh, it was pot butter (menyn pot) that had been preserved in brine in an earthenware container. If the men wanted more of anything, they knocked the table and the female maids would get them whatever they wanted.

The maids ate after the men had finished. The main ingredient of the midday meal was boiled salted beef. The master went to Caernarfon to purchase the meat; he bought about 70 lbs at a time and then cut it up and salted it. Potatoes and butter were also served regularly. Sunday dinner was the biggest treat when fresh meat was served with potatoes cooked in the oven (tatws popty).

In the afternoon tea was taken down in the pitcher to the labourers and they drank this with bread and butter and perhaps some jam (cynyswyd). The men finished work at seven o'clock and they came to the kitchen for their supper which was porridge, made with oatmeal, and bread and butter and milk.

Mary Elin continued to work in service until she married in 1907.

The records in this section are very limited but we can be sure that most girls and women would find themselves in situations similar to those described here. The cases noted in the Bastardy Minute books shine a light on a hidden and distressing aspect of domestic service when men took advantage of their servants and the women were then left to live with the consequences.

Chapter 6

A Detested Occupation

In the earlier sections we have considered the work that was carried out by servants in very different environments and established that the image of domestic service presented in contemporary dramas does not fit the reality for the majority of women. In this section we will look at the main features that characterised the nature of life in service and the reasons why women turned to other occupations if they had the choice.

The central feature of employment in domestic service was that the servant was taken into the home of her employer and was obliged to abide by the rules and regulations of that household. The employer had absolute authority over his or her servants while they lived under his or her roof. Subservience and deference were the qualities that employers demanded of their servants.

The law added force to the unwritten principle and this came out clearly in the case of Turner v. Mason (1845). Ann Turner, who was a servant, asked her employer for permission to visit her mother whom she thought was dying from a seizure. When she was refused this request she decided to absent herself anyway with the result that she was dismissed. When the case came to court, the employer's action was upheld on the grounds that it was considered doubtful 'whether any service to be rendered to any person than the master would suffice as an excuse for defying a master's lawful command'. It was therefore established as 'a master's province to regulate the conduct of his domestic servant'.

In this private domain, interference in domestic matters was positively discouraged in the moral climate of the time. Domestic servants had very little bargaining power and the potential always existed for employers to take advantage of servants. This could mean abuse, cruelty, overwork, starvation and even murder.

Historians have documented shocking examples of brutality towards servants by employers. For example, Pamela Horn gives an example of a fourteen year old orphan from Bideford in Devon who was engaged by a farmer, Robert Bird, as a general servant in September 1849. Her mistress started to accuse her of dishonesty and began to treat her cruelly and deprive her of food. She was subjected to systematic beatings which, by January 1850, had proved fatal. A post-mortem examination, carried out three days after her death revealed the extent of her injuries: 'There was a vast number of wounds and - abscesses of some standing on the arms; the nails of the fingers on the left hand had been gone for some time, and the bone of the middle-finger was protruding, the result, probably, of frost bite and a low state of the system. On the right hip was a slough as large as the palm of the hand . . . The stomach was perfectly empty.' The employers were taken to court for the murder but because they could not establish which one of the couple had administered the fatal blow, the jury returned a verdict of "Not Guilty". Later in the year the same employers were indicted on three charges of assault arising out of the same facts. They were convicted on this occasion but were only given a sentence of two years imprisonment. [1]

Guidebooks and manuals that gave advice to servants

---

[1] P. Horn, op cit., p.113

presented a positive view of paternalistic relations between employers and employees. Lynne Haims shows that this was sometimes done on religious grounds, for example, stressing that Christ too had been a servant and that service was an act of sanctification and inequality of station had been divinely arranged. [2]

The author of the 'Dictionary of Daily Wants' also stressed the necessity for inequality when he gave this advice to servants, 'Harsh expressions and hasty words occasionally addressed by an employer to his servant, should be overlooked instead of being resented. The servant should be cheerful and willing and content with the station which has been assigned him, he should remember that there must of necessity be some grades in life lower than others; and, in order that he may reconcile himself to his lot with that of thousands who are much worse situated than himself; responsibilities which attach themselves to the higher spheres of society'. [3]

Employers assumed they could exercise control over all areas of their servants' lives. There are examples, for instance, of employers giving servants new names because they did not like, or could not pronounce their original name. There are examples of this happening to Welsh servants because their names were difficult to pronounce. Some employers called all their servants by the same name to save them having to remember new names when new appointments were made.

What clothes were worn was another area that employers tried to influence. Servants were encouraged to wear plain clothes and discouraged from following fashion and wearing jewellery. During the craze for crinolines, it was common for employers to specify 'no crinolines'.

---

[2] L. Haimes, op cit., p.61
[3] 'Dictionary of Daily Wants', (1860), by the Editor of 'Enquire Within Upon Everything', pp. 666-667

Religion was another important way in which control was exercised over servants. 'No Irish Need Apply' was sometimes written on adverts for servants because employers did not want to employ any Catholics. Attendance at morning or evening prayers was also made compulsory in some households as well as regular attendance at church or chapel on Sundays.

Servants were treated very much like children and disobedience and insubordination could be dealt with harshly. Servants were also constrained by the fact that they needed character references from former employers before they could secure another position. Because the law worked in the interests of the employers, domestic servants who were taken to court could be treated severely, for example in cases of petty theft or alcoholism. There is a local example in the Plas Coch papers of two female servants being taken to court accused of stealing wine. [4]

Domestic servants lived where they worked and for this reason there was no clear distinction between work and leisure. No provision was made for the leisure time of servants. In some large households there were servants' halls where servants could go if they had any free time during their working day. However, in most cases servants had to take what rest they could get in the kitchen where the furniture was usually minimal. Mrs Panton, in 'From Kitchen to Garret,' advised against installing carpets in any of the servants' rooms. [5]

Sleeping accommodation for servants was usually basic and no consideration was given for the fact that servants might have needed comfortable rooms to relax in after doing a hard day's work. Servants also worked incredibly long hours which made their leisure time extremely limited. Holidays and days off away from the premises

---

[4] Bangor University, Plas Coch MSS., 4048
[5] P.Horn, op cit., p.97

were also very limited. The subject of free time for servants is dealt with in Beeton's Domestic Service Guide which states that, in the country 'it was customary for servants to have a week allowed them once a year', and that they should not expect any other holiday although it was considered that few people would deny 'a day to an industrious willing servant'. However, in London 'no yearly holiday is granted; but every six weeks or so a whole day is allowed'.

The leisure time allocated to servants in the most generous households, even at the end of the century, was normally restricted to a fortnight's holiday each year, plus a half day every Sunday, one day off per month and an evening out weekly. Many fared far worse than this.

The nature of the work in domestic service, coupled with the shortage of free time, set limits on the social interactions that were possible for servants. This was most marked in the case of the general servant who worked on her own in the household. Her only social contact would be with people who delivered goods to the house. Lack of companionship, the monotony of her work and poor conditions of employment sometimes led women to take up prostitution as an alternative occupation.

Servants in larger households had the advantage of working with other people and this could open up the possibility of forming close friendships. In some establishments, the authority of the employers extended to the organisation of their servants' leisure time. Servants often complained that in lieu of more leisure time, employers organised activities for them which were considered to be useful and healthy.

Employers also had strict control over who visited their servants. This was often done with a view to protecting servants from undesirable influences. Mrs Beeton gave this advice to mistresses:

'A lady should never allow herself to forget the important duty of watching over the moral and physical welfare of those beneath her roof. Without seeming unduly inquisitive, she can always learn something of their acquaintances and holiday occupation, and should, when necessary, warn them against the dangers and evils of bad company. An hour should be fixed, usually 10 or 9 p.m. after which no servants should be allowed to stay out.'

It is likely, of course, that servants found ways around the restrictions that were placed upon them by their employers.

Clearly situations varied greatly and some employers did take care of their servants and there are examples of long service identified here that suggest that great loyalty could be shown by both servants and employers. A local example from Rhuddgaer, Dwyran shows that the employer paid to have a portrait photograph taken of their housekeeper, Ellen Owen. She is described as the 'faithful housekeeper' and the photograph was taken by A&G Taylor describing himself as 'Photographer to the Queen'. [6] This suggests that some money was spent in doing this and that Ellen Owen meant a great deal to the family. The employer William Humphrey Owen (1825-1896) from a shipping family was a JP and High Sheriff of Anglesey. Someone in the family was clearly interested in photography because there are a number of very interesting and high quality photographs from the mid nineteenth century in the collection and this is very unusual. [7]

---

[6] Llangefni Archives, Rhuddgaer Papers, WDD/2301
[7] Cover photograph WDD/2245; House WDD/1825; Staff WDD/1827; Housekeeper WDD/2301.

Rhuddgaer House, parish of Llangeinwen, Dwyran,
Anglesey (No date)
Courtesy of Anglesey Archives, Llangefni

Group Photograph of Staff at Rhuddgaer
(No date but likely to be 1850s)
Courtesy of Anglesey Archives, Llangefni

Photograph of Ellen Owen, Housekeeper to
William Humphrey Owen (No date)
Courtesy of Anglesey Archives, Llangefni

The Yorke family of Erddig are also very well known for
taking painted portraits and photographs of their servants
over a very long period and these serve as an exceptionally
valuable source for historians.[8]

Sian Evans makes the point that the average life
expectancy of a man in the mid-nineteenth century was 41,
and that of a woman 44, but many working class people
died earlier in the newly industrialised and unregulated
factories, mills and mines. [9] Domestic service for all its

---

[8] Many are included in M. Waterson, op cit.
[9] S. Evans, op cit., p. 169

restrictions and long hours of repetitive and tedious work did at least, in the better households, offer a degree of protection from these extreme conditions and some servants were able to save some money and good employers did make provision for old age for long serving staff. [10]

Not all servants were so fortunate, and the narrow and restrictive nature of life in service contributed to the eventual decline of this occupation as women opted for work that offered more regular hours and which did not entail living on employer's premises.

Marriage was one way to escape the need to 'live in' and young women in service tended to marry earlier than women in other occupations. The skills gained from working in domestic service and their knowledge about how things should be done properly in the home gave women servants some prospects and a certain kind of status.

The difficulties in finding servants led many employers to use newspapers to advertise for staff. [11] The 'servant problem' became a topic of interest in the press as the extracts below illustrate:

Cardiff Times 24 January 1880

'Ladies Column
Servants were once mistreated and there was a celebrated strike of servants a few years ago. The other extreme has now been reached and some suggest that a strike of mistresses would now be in order. Present servants are incompetent and inexperienced compared with their predecessors. The position of a mistress in an ordinary English household in the present day is anything but an enviable one'. Faithful servants should now be prized like

---

[10] Ibid., p.170
[11] I am most grateful to Dr Neil Evans for his generosity in sharing these valuable press cuttings with me from south Wales taken from his own research.

precious treasures. To return to the former dictatorial position would not be desirable but there should be reconciliation.'

Cardiff Times 2 July 1892

'Domestic Service
Social philosophers are observing among girls of the working class a growing distaste for domestic service – a distaste which is intensified by the spread of education. They prefer lower wages and the greater freedom/lesser servility of working in a shop or a factory. The factory girl has many problems; it is harder work and the money not as good and she has difficulty finding good accommodation. Despite superior conditions domestic service is becoming less attractive; it is not the degradation to which girls object, but the confinement and control. Servants must be treated in the same manner as other workers.

Obviously if servants are not to become extinct, more liberty must be allowed them and they must be treated from the same standpoint as other workers. The hours must be regulated, and mistresses must make arrangements by which the servant can know what time she can have to herself. She must come on duty at a certain hour, and the old slavish conditions of homage will have to be modified. Because a man is hired to drive a carriage that is no reason why he should touch his cap to the master and all his friends, and because a maid is employed to open the front door that is no reason why she should be forced to wear a cap, and otherwise be distinguished by a badge of servitude.'

During the course of the century, a change can be detected in relations between employers and their employees. Paternalism was slowly being replaced by a contract system. While many aspects of the traditional relationship between master and servant continued, particularly the paternal role of the master, other elements were changing.

The old style paternalism of the aristocracy had placed servants in a subordinate position but, in an ironic way, they were also viewed as members of the family and under the protective wing of the patriarch.

Women's magazines and manuals were also promoting the idea that servants should be treated like any other workers. This assumed a more contractual basis to the relationship between employers and employees. Other elements such as rationalisation and efficiency became more apparent. This took the form in domestic service, as it did in the factories, of stricter rules and regulations about time-keeping and more careful supervision. The writer in the Cardiff Times is promoting the need for a more contractual understanding between employers and their servants as a way of preventing women from voting with their feet and finding new forms of employment.

It is difficult to assess how these debates actually affected the work of servants. It was unlikely that the burden of work would lessen and domestic service had for so long been laden with paternalistic assumptions, it is impossible to see this changing to any great extent. Lynne Haims has summed this up very succinctly in saying, 'Often the transition took the form of an employer's fulfilling a strict contractual agreement, while expecting the deference associated with older paternalism'. [12]

Major changes were taking place in Britain at the beginning of the twentieth century and 1910 has been identified by some writers as a symbolic turning point. Nineteenth century relations between employers and their workers were strained as a result of the growing strength of trades unions, the success of the Labour Party in the 1906 election and the Liberal government's promotion of greater state intervention for welfare assistance with its 'People's Budget'.

---

[12] L. Haimes, op. cit., p. 317⁹ S. Evans, op cit., p. 169

One historian, Dr Selina Todd, has offered a very positive view of this period saying that, 'Between 1910 and 1945 the working class transformed themselves from the poor into people. They did not all want to become respectable as middle-class social investigators hoped: many wanted freedom from want and anxiety, and took advantage of a bit of security or financial credit to have a good time when they could. [13] In 1910 and in 1923 domestic servants remained the largest single group of working people in Britain. [14] The 'servant problem' and relations between servants and their employers in Todd's view reflect British society in microcosm as workers became more confident in expressing their demands. The concerns expressed by employers centred around the fact that servants were increasingly acting like industrial workers. In this way they were identifying themselves with the interests of the working class as opposed to the interests of their employers. [15]

There were attempts too to form a union of domestic servants. In 1910, the Domestic Workers' Union of Great Britain was formed in London and a similar organisation was established in Glasgow in response to correspondence in the press expressing the dissatisfaction felt by so many servants. [16] The National Federation of Women Workers was formed in 1906 and in 1919 the first branch of domestic workers in Wales was established in Colwyn Bay. These organisations experienced difficulties in sustaining support due to the private nature of the work.

Debates about the relationship between servants and their employers took centre stage again around the introduction of the Insurance Act (1911). The fear of illness and old age had always weighed heavily on domestic servants and

---

[13] S. Todd, The People, The Rise and Fall of the Working Class, (2014)
[14] Ibid., p.14
[15] Ibid., p.21
[16] P. Horn, op cit., p. 179

there are tragic examples of women being turned away from their employers when illness struck. If servants were unable to save for old age, the workhouse was often the only option open to them. Joseph Chamberlain giving evidence to the Royal Commission on the Aged Poor in 1893 stated that 'no one would employ a servant past 50 years of age and accordingly, almost by the necessity of the case, they will have to go to the workhouse'. [17]

The Insurance Act proposed by the Liberal Government promised benefits and free medical assistance in times of illness based on a system of contributions by both employers and workers. Each employer would pay 3d. per week in tax for a female servant (4d for a male) and this was to be matched by contributions by the servants themselves. Medical bills would then be covered and 7/6d per week could be claimed for six months in illness and 5 shillings a week if permanently unable to work. Servants would make payments at the post office and receive stamps in return, saved in a book.

The proposals fuelled a passionate debate from all quarters of society. Protest organisations were formed and at the first meeting of the 'Servants Tax Registers Defence Organisation, the Chancellor was likened to an agent of revolutionary terror, a 'tyrant, gagger, guillotiner, attempting to do what the worst kings in the darkest ages of history failed to do'. [18] Local and national newspapers had a field day as the quotation below shows. The Daily Mail fuelled a vicious campaign based on misinformation claiming that servants would lose their jobs as a result of the Bill.

'Her position is positively changed for the worse. In present circumstances, if she is ill her mistress provides her with medical attendance, pays her wages, and cares for

---

[17] P. Horn, op cit., p. 186

[18] L. Lethbridge, *Servants, A Downstairs View of Twentieth-century Britain*, (2013) p. 114

till she is well. Under the Bill the servant will run the risk of being required to shift for herself in illness. She will be granted medical attendance by an overworked and underpaid insurance doctor, and given a wretched pittance of 7s.6d. a week to meet the cost of her maintenance. Nor is this all the mischief that will be caused by these clauses of the Bill. There are thousands of families too poor to pay the new tax of 26s for a servant; and thus will be obliged to do without a domestic. A great increase in the number of unemployed servants is therefore a certainty.' [19]

The debate over the Insurance Act was discussed locally and there are a number of entries on the topic in the North Wales Chronicle in 1911. [20]

For example, on November 24th this article stated:

'Objections to the Bill

Why Mistresses Don't Want It

The Bill imposes a fresh tax of 26s a year for each servant upon households that are already heavily burdered.

Thousands of servants will leave their situations rather than allow mistresses to deduct 13s from their wages.

There are too many poor women in this class who really cannot afford 26s. The tax is the same on them as on people who can pay it without suffering. Widows, nurses and spinsters who are compelled to go out and make a meagre living – just enough to keep them in food and shelter – and have to engage a girl to do their housework, will have to

---

[19] From P.Horn, op cit., p.183
[20] Gwynedd Archives, Caernarfon.

deprive themselves of necessaries or do their own housework.

Why Servants Oppose It

The Bill is no use to a servant in a home where she is kindly treated.
They know that their mistresses cannot afford it, and there will be enmity between the two as to which of them shall contribute a tax that neither want to pay for 'benefits' which are despised by both.

In the light of the earlier discussion about the development of a new type of contract between servants and their employers there is a reference in the discussion stating that:

'The Bill is another step in the direction of making the domestic servant a 'workman' and giving her status and respect which has never really been hers.'

There is also a very long list of the names of mistresses and servants who oppose the proposals. They include:

Penrhyn Castle with a list of servants
A M White (housekeeper)
M A Hughes (sewing maid)
L Flatman (housemaid)
Kate Holmes
Emily Gibbs (housemaid)
Edith Hall (still room maid)
(It is interesting to note here again that most of the names suggest that the servants were English.)

There are a number of entries of houses around Menai View Terrace, College Road and Holyhead Road revealing just how many lone, 'general servants' there were in that area.

There is also a notice of a public meeting that has been organised in Penrhyn Hall, Bangor, November 28th 1911 to 'Protest against this Tax being inflicted upon Mistresses and Servants'.

For obvious reasons, Lloyd George was used by cartoonists and critics and the image of the 'insurance stamp' was frequently used.

This example from the North Wales Chronicle, Friday, December 15, 1911 is particularly amusing in its depiction of Lloyd George in an apron.

From North Wales Chronicle 1911
Courtesy of Gwynedd Archives, Caernarfon

There were also supporters of the Act. On the same page as the list of mistresses and servants mentioned above there was a section headed:

'Lady Lewis and the Servants' Tax
We have received a letter from Lady Lewis, Belmont, stating that she was asked 'to sign a Form of Protest ......
and I cannot accept the statements made on the Protest form as a full and true description of the provision of the Bill; and further, I agree with Mr Chamberlain and other prominent Conservatives and Liberals, that this Bill, as a whole, is calculated to bring joy and help in time of need to many thousands of those who suffer'.

It is interesting that servants were protesting about legislation that was intended to help their situation. The newspapers had clearly led a campaign of misinformation that drew on arguments around the need to maintain the status quo between servants and their employers and servants. Clearly, there would have been some genuine concern about the financial impact on them but there was likely to be an element of needing to be seen to be on the same side as their employer. It would have been very difficult for servants to stand up to their employers if they were opposing the proposals.

The Act was passed and by 1915 the Domestic Servants Insurance Society that was formed to help servants manage the new Act had a membership of 75,000. [21] The scare stories that had been promoted by the press did not happen. Selina Todd has suggested that the Liberal Government maintained their position on the legislation because they saw it as a means of protecting the occupation from decline as well as offering a minimal degree of protection and encouraging workers to save for

---

[21] L. Lethbridge, op. cit., p115

their future. [22] For some of course, the Act did not go far enough but it was significant step in establishing a marker for welfare reform.

The debate around domestic service as a whole and the problem of recruiting servants continued in the period prior to the First World War. The extracts below are Cardiff based but they reflect a more general phenomenon that applied across Wales. [23] The South Wales Daily News interviewed employers and servants and these are some reasons given for the shortage of servants.

South Wales Daily News October 30 1912

'Insurance Act Blamed
Other ladies who were interviewed supplied our representative with a variety of reasons for the shortage of servants. One lady declared it was "owing to Lloyd George's wicked Insurance Act", another summed up the question in two words, "Picture shows", and a third said "Socialism", and a fourth "Free education," and a fifth expressed the original if somewhat enigmatic opinion that girls were "getting too flighty" for domestic service.'

In the midst of this fierce debate, one mistress expressed this rather extreme view in the Western Mail saying, 'the lack of servants will lead to the extinction of the nation – young wives are not going to undertake the responsibilities of motherhood when they cannot get servants on reasonable terms . . . no maid, no motherhood.'

Servants themselves got involved in the debate around domestic service and for the first time we start to hear the voices of women who had previously been invisible.

---

[22] S. Todd, op. cit., p.23
[23] From Dr Neil Evans

South Wales Daily News, October 31 1912

'The Servants' Loneliness
Sir, - In regard to your article of the 30th inst. on the shortage of servants, 1 wonder if you would be good enough to print a few reasons why this is so. In the first place, take the loneliness of a girl placed like I am, and like the majority of servants in Cardiff where there is only one kept. 1 wonder how many mistresses would like the life of living from Sunday to Thursday without seeing any of her friends, never getting a breath of fresh air, and having every meal by herself. Every day is just like another- the same work over and over again until one gets heartily sick of it.

Again, there is the supposed degradation. We are looked down on as a class, as something low, even by the smallest shop girl, while people a little higher treat us as though we had no intelligence whatever, as merely beings with a pair of arms and feet to fetch and carry and do as we are told, with no prospect of being anything else.

Of course 1 know these things cannot be remedied, and that is why I say there is no wonder that people complain they cannot get good servants. If 1 could have afforded or had a home where 1 could have been trained for something better rewarded, 1 should never have had the hateful task of signing myself.'

South Wales Daily News November 1 1912

Cardiff Girl's Experience
Sir, - Being a domestic servant, 1 was greatly impressed with the excuses given by the ladies seen by your reporter for the shortage of servants. Let me tell you what I think after having been four months in service at Cardiff. I consider 1 am treated more like a slave than a human being - driven from 6 am until eleven and twelve at night, eating my own meals while running about waiting on others. As

to freedom, if treated properly while in the house we should not require so much outing. Situations are often misrepresented (as my present one was to me), and if a girl cannot stand the hardships she is turned away without a reference. All that is left for her then is the streets, as a lady's word is always taken before a servant's. If the higher class would only give a little more consideration to their servants and treat them as they would like to be treated, they would find themselves the employers of willing and contented servants.

MARGARET CARDIFF'

There is a confidence in many of the letters written by servants that they are deserving of better than they have been offered in the past. An important factor too is that the debate about domestic service was now out in the open. The problem in the nineteenth-century was that servants had been hidden away in the homes of their employers. It was not territory that people could easily talk about or criticise. Mistresses are given a bad press in the letters written by servants at this time and the private concerns of middle-class families are therefore becoming public. This reflected a change in attitudes towards the middle-class. Servants appear to be very aware of their own class position but are asserting their right, nonetheless, to be treated fairly and with respect.

The outbreak of the First World War has been seen as a watershed for women because of the occupations they were asked to take up for the war effort. As in other parts of Great Britain, women in Wales were employed in areas that had previously been dominated by men and the sight of women driving buses and working in munitions factories started to change perceptions about women and what they were capable of achieving. These images were far removed from the nineteenth-century 'angel in the home'. The debate around women's suffrage was also challenging perceptions about women's roles in society.

Women were praised for their efforts during the war and described in glowing terms in the press. The Daily Chronicle ran an article titled 'Our Amazons' and referred to the debt the nation owed to these 'heroic women' – a debt likened to that owed to its soldiers and sailors.[24]

These positive images of women were soon to change. When the war ended women were no longer needed in wartime occupations and men returning from war were seen to be re-claiming their rights to paid employment. Ex-war workers were entitled to an 'out of work donation' of 25 shillings for thirteen weeks, first payable in December 1918. In order to receive this benefit they had to be available for work and attend the labour exchange daily. If women who had been active the war were offered work as domestic servants they were expected to accept and if they refused, were struck off the register. This applied even in those cases where the wage offered was less than the amount given in benefits. The women who had been so admired for their efforts in wartime were now presented in the press as shirkers for refusing to enter domestic service.

The following extract from the Western Mail in January 1919 illustrates the point:

'In the case of women, however, the hope of meeting the demand for 'suitable' employment seems hopeless, chiefly because these women war workers were, prior to 1914, either employed in domestic service, to which they will not return at the wages offered to them, or were at home with their parents.

During the war they have had artificially inflated high wages, and they have not a sufficient grasp of economic

---

[24] For further discussion see D. Beddoe, *Back to Home and Duty, Women Between the Wars 1918-1939* (1989)

factors to appreciate that the country's post-war industries, now in a state of flux, cannot absorb them on the old abnormal wage terms. Human nature being what it is they decline to accept anything offered to them as 'suitable' and stick to the 25 shilling a week donation, on which they continue to enjoy their holiday. Thousands of young Welsh women from South Wales areas went to the large munition districts. Now they have returned and claimed the donations, and unless new industries are established or old industries extended and developed these women cannot possibly be absorbed and the time is approaching when they must realise that domestic service, which they were originally engaged in, must again be their main source of livelihood, that is if they want to do anything at all. Seaside places and other holiday centres throughout the country are said to be now reaping a harvest from young women who are out for a good time on their savings as munitions workers, and their donations.'

Women who took the dole were also described as the 'unemployed in fur coats'. The Evening Standard ran an article headed 'Slackers with State Pay' – with sub heading 'want luxurious days to continue' saying:

'Their wages have run up to £2 and £3 a week. Fur coats, high topped kid boots, gramophones, every night off, and Sundays in many cases free, have given them higher morale and not readily, especially with weekly gifts of 25s for walking to the employment exchanges, are they going to take on the shackles of domestic work.'

The letters and articles were numerous and sentiments expressed vociferously. Domestic service emerges as a detested occupation but women seemed powerless to release themselves from the stranglehold it continued to have over their lives. The debates were also underpinned by assumptions about what roles were considered appropriate for women in society. The insistence by some commentators that domestic service was the most suitable occupation for women was based on a generalised view that women should continue to be content with their role as home-makers. Although the involvement of women in the First World War had signalled a change in attitudes, these were quickly ignored and the backlash after the war served to force women back into the home or domestic service. Selina Todd makes the point that, 'those women who found themselves forced back into domestic service bitterly resented it'. The Women's Industrial Council sent out questionnaires to over 500 servants in 1914 and found that 'servants often speak sadly of themselves as a class apart'. [25] They referred to the loneliness, long hours of work and poor conditions that servants experienced in their places of work.

This debate about the 'servant problem' was occurring within the context of a bigger deliberation about the role of women in society. 'Time and Tide', the weekly magazine run by Lady Rhondda promoting equal rights for women, also debated the issue. Again, servants in their own voices expressed very strong feelings about their experiences and hatred of domestic service. In its editorial, it concluded that only financial desperation could force women back into service and that no amount of moral outrage could persuade them ' that (their) only hope of virtue lies in self-sacrifice', the quality that is so strongly associated with a life in service.

Women were clearly looking for other employment opportunities where they could. In one employment exchange for example only one woman out of three thousand entered her name as willing to enter domestic

---

[25] S. Todd, op. cit., p.40

service. But as was pointed out in 'Time and Tide', large numbers of women were unable to find alternatives and domestic service stubbornly remained a key employer of women. In 1851 9.8 per cent of the total female population of England and Wales was employed in domestic service. By 1871 the figure had increased to 12.8 per cent. Thereafter the figure declined but as late as 1931, 7.7 per cent of the female population was still employed in this occupation. This represented 23 per cent of occupied females in 1931 (total 1,332,224). It is likely by this date that fewer women were employed as 'live-in' servants and others would have been employed in family shops, cafes and restaurants but an estimated 800,000 continued to live with their employers.

Rosemary Scadden recorded interviews with women who had been domestic servants between the wars and their stories are as tragic as those discussed earlier here. Economic necessity was often the driver and leaving home was always heartbreaking. [26]

'Hilda
When I was seventeen, things became very bad underground. It would have been about 1930, I suppose. Some days they worked and some days they were not able to work. I wanted to help and, like most girls in the same situation, we had no alternative but to go to seek work elsewhere. We weren't trained for anything really, having left school at fourteen, but we knew how to work domestically, so we found work away from the Valleys. That's all we could do really. We didn't know anything else.

My cousin from Maerdy was a little older and she was already away. She said there was a place for me, at the Red House in Surrey. So I went to Surrey as an under housemaid.'

---

[26] R. Scadden, No Job For A Little Girl, (2013)

'Miriam

I remember the day I left Pontypridd, I broke my heart! I can remember sitting up in bed. My mother used to have cats and I was sitting with one cat in one arm and one cat in the other and my father came to kiss me goodbye. He didn't want me to go. He didn't want any of his children to leave home, but there was nothing for us. I mean the government didn't give you money to look after you then. I was sitting up in bed breaking my heart.'

Ceinwen was sent away to work in 1932 when she was fourteen years old:

'My father saw me off at the station. I was sobbing my heart out as soon as the train pulled out of the station. One woman wanted to call him, to fetch me home. I nearly broke my heart, I did. I'd never been to London. I didn't know what to expect, did I? And I swore that if ever I got married, my children would never do it. Never! They would never skivvy for anyone else, and thank God they didn't have to.

I can't remember anyone meeting me at Paddington, but there must have been someone there. I was the only Welsh girl in the house and they couldn't pronounce my name, so I went as 'Jane'. Every letter I'd have from home I used to take to the toilet where I'd be sobbing my heart out. My mother used to say, 'Be a brave girl'. But I broke my heart, I did. I'd never wish it on anybody.'

Ceinwen said that she was homesick the whole time in the two years she spent in London and twelve of the twenty women interviewed described their feelings of depression at leaving and living away from home.

A detested occupation it may have been but large numbers of women were unable to escape its clutches. Domestic service casts a long shadow over women's history and there is great sadness in thinking about lost opportunities and potential for those women who spent their lives looking after others and had so little time for their own interests and pleasures. These hard-working women gave years of their lives to people who showed them little appreciation. This was the reality of life below the stairs and what we see in period dramas is very far off the mark when it comes to the experience of the majority of women and girls in service and the romanticised view presented to us does a disservice to their struggles and sacrifices.

Further Reading:

M. Arthur, *Lost Voices of the Edwardians*, (Harper, 2007).

D. Beddoe, *Back to Home and Duty*, (Pandora Press, 1989).

J. Burnett, *Useful Toil, Autobiographies of Working People from the 1820s to the 1930s*, (Routledge, 2nd edition, 1994).

L. Delap, *Knowing Their Place: Domestic Service in Twentieth Century Britain*, (Cambridge, 2011).

S. Evans, *Life Below the Stairs in the Victorian and Edwardian Country House*, (National Trust Books, 2011).

P. Horn, *The Rise and Fall of the Victorian Servant*, (Sutton, 1975).

A.V. John, (ed.), *Our Mother's Land; Chapters in Welsh Women's History 1830–1939*, (University of Wales Press, 2nd edition, 2011).

L. Lethbridge, *Servants: A Downstairs View of Twentieth-century Britain*, (Bloomsbury, 2013).

A. Maloney, *Life Below the Stairs: True Lives of Edwardian Servants*, (London, 2011).

P. Sambrook, *Keeping their Place: Domestic Service in the Country Home*, (History Press, 2005).

R. Scadden, *No Job for a Little Girl, Voices from Domestic Service*, (Gomer, 2013).

S. Todd, *The People, The Rise and Fall of the Working Class*, (John Murray, 2015).